Quantum Boost

Using Quantum Computing to Supercharge Your Business

Brian T. Lenahan

Acclaim for Quantum Boost

“Brian Lenahan's book lays out a roadmap for how to incorporate quantum into your roadmap and achieve quantum readiness in advance of this transformation.”

- *Paul Lipman, Chief Commercial Officer, Cold Quanta*

“Vital to have a "business-focused" view of this topic so executives can understand why they need to be considering quantum computing now.”

- *Paulo Cuomo, Director of Operations, Brit Insurance*

“This book will be tremendously useful.”

- *David Isaac, The Quantum News*

“Very impressive Brian Lenahan, you’re always at the leading edge of technologies”

- *Bert Kaminski, Director, Legal - Google Cloud*

Quantum Boost

Using Quantum Computing to Supercharge Your Business

Brian T. Lenahan

Aquitaine Innovation Advisors

Toronto

www.aquitaineinnovationadvisors.com

Designed by Brian T. Lenahan

Library of Congress Cataloging-in-Publication Data
Names: Lenahan, Brian T., 1963- author;
Title: Quantum Boost – Using Quantum Computing to Supercharge Your Business / Brian Lenahan,
Description: First edition. | Toronto: Aquitaine Innovation Advisors, 2021. | Includes bibliographical references and index.
Identifiers: ISBN 978-1-989478-12-7 (paperback) | ISBN 978-1-989478-13-4 (ebook)
Subjects: LCSH: Human-machine systems. | Quantum Computing. | Automation.

Cover design: Brian Lenahan

First Edition: May 2021

10 9 8 7 6 5 4 3 2 1

Table of Contents

Dedication

When life constantly throws up barriers and there's no one around to support you, look deep inside for your own inspiration, to do it anyway. This book is dedicated to those who just do it anyway.

Acknowledgements

Inspiration comes from many sources and for me it's sports athletes Jim Brown, Larry Bird, Magic Johnson and Tom Brady. Each of them hardworking, persistent, intelligent, and believed in themselves despite so many others. Thanks for your videos making the writing process so much easier. Thanks also to country music, Electric Light Orchestra, SpaceX launches and NBA highlights on YouTube for making the writing experience so much more comfortable with inspiration breaks.

Thanks also go to those pioneers in the universe of quantum computing for lighting the torches for others to follow. Appreciation also for CERN Quantum Technology Initiative/University of Oviedo and TU Delft University for their excellent educational programs on quantum computing and to my colleagues at Quantum London who have supported this book's journey.

Thanks to my editors who provided wonderful feedback and direction to make this a much better book.

Introduction

"Get ready to think outside a box you didn't know existed" – Charlie Bennett (IBM Fellow at IBM Research)

In 2017, I started a company called Aquitaine Innovation Advisors and for a very clear reason. The business leaders in my network were hearing about this relatively new technology, artificial intelligence or AI, yet were uncertain what it meant for them in terms of opportunities, barriers, and competitive advantage. Having a background in AI through previous work and completing MIT's AI Strategy for Business program combined with over 20 years in business, I felt comfortable sharing with these leaders and guiding them on the AI journey.

Fast forward to 2020, when another 'new' technology, quantum computing, made a substantial leap in its maturity and evolution. Once again, business leaders began asking questions about quantum computing's relevance to their research, operations, simulations, optimization questions, and the advantages over classical computing. I was excited to guide them on the quantum journey with my research and educational interactions with CERN in Switzerland and with Delft University in the Netherlands.

The world of quantum computing can be highly complex in understanding the underlying quantum mechanics, physics, math, hardware let alone how it might apply to you. Writing a book for business people to assist in that understanding just made sense to me especially in terms of the practical applications of this new, evolving technology. Gartner said in June 2020 that “quantum computers will drive the discovery of new, patentable chemicals, drugs and materials, but remain a decade into the future.” Do we need to wait until 2030 for viable quantum uses? The answer in this book is a resounding ‘No’.

My research for this book extends worldwide, whether through first-person interviews, academic and lab research, public sources or mass media. I'm one of those curiosity hounds who reads several articles a day on a subject and files them away for 'sometime soon in the future.' That sometime is now in Quantum Boost.

The Quantum for Business 2020 (or Q2B20) conference held in December of that year reinforced for me the growing world of quantum computing applications to business. It shaped my way of thinking about how I could convey the realities and complexities of quantum computing in a way that made sense to businesspeople. My goal in this book is to share the fundamental physics that makes quantum computing powerful and an interesting topic to study and its relation to business success in the future. This book is intended for business and information technology leaders and participants who want to understand how this new incredible technology is expected to impact their department, company, industry, strategy choices, and future.

Today's written word covering quantum computing speaks most often to the underlying quantum mechanics, physics, algorithm development, and hardware. Yet little has been written about how businesses can leverage such a futuristic, advanced technology in real business applications. I hope to inspire the reader to look outside their industry and IT departments' current focus to gain at least a surface understanding of quantum computing and some of the applications in current day use and the possible opportunities in the future.

Robert Schoekopf, Sterling Professor of Applied Physics at Yale University, once said, "If you had brought an iPhone to someone 25 years ago, they would have called you a wizard." In 2021, the same applies to quantum computing technology. It seems too futuristic to be practical and complex to be understood. When business leaders have so many competing priorities, how can one add such an unknown quantity to the mix?

If you read the "Why This Book and Why Now?" section, you'll comprehend the urgency of understanding quantum computing at some practical level to incorporate into any firm's technology strategy. To help readers on the journey, this book begins with an overview of what quantum computing is, moves into a timeline of the progress of this technology, and then, a high-level dive into the subjects of quantum physics and mechanics.

If data is the fuel of business, research, and academics today, then quantum computing is the engine of the future, and artificial intelligence is the set of instructions layered on top of the quantum infrastructure and powered by data. The combination of AI and quantum computing promises to be a staggering leap forward for business.

If you've read anything about quantum computing in the media, you've likely heard about quantum supremacy (tied to a dispute between Google and IBM), so we explore that topic, as well as a review of quantum maturity and the potential convergence of technologies. We also explore existing vendors and individual business and thought leaders in the quantum space.

In Section 1, Quantum Boost finishes with major categories like the global landscape, simulations, and the new quantum networks and internet. Section 2 focuses squarely on how quantum computing can be 'put to work' with impacts on the workforce of the future and specific use cases in pharmaceuticals, manufacturing, power generation, security, finance, retail, and traffic flow. We conclude by sharing insights into what the future holds for quantum computing.

There are many more steps beyond reading this book to embed quantum computing in your company culture. Make sure you take advantage of the over 50 pages of resource material in the appendices including glossaries, list of industry players, vendors, and reference documentation. Get specific on what you need to know and then check out the links in the Notes section.

My goal in writing this book is to make quantum computing more accessible to you, the business person, regardless of level. As a manager in a large financial institution, I was always looking for ways to automate functions. As an executive, I pushed for investments in technology that would see repetitive activities automated and knowledgeable employees move on to more value-add activities. Quantum computing for business is yet another way to accomplish the technology evolution within your organization. I hope in reading Quantum Boost, you and your teams will become quantum ready.

SECTION 1 Quantum Computing Overview

Chapter 1

Why This Book & Why Now?

"In certain classes of problems, where outcomes are governed by unintuitive and surprising relationships among the different input factors, quantum computers have the potential to better predict that distribution thereby leading to a more correct answer."

- Tony Uttley, President, Honeywell Quantum

Today, as of 2021, if you're a billion-dollar and higher company, quantum computing is already a "powerful tool" according to Canadian company D-Wave Systems. Due to the size and complexity of such large organizations' problems, quantum computers are ideal for such challenges. Financial institutions like JP Morgan Chase, pharmaceutical companies in a consortium like QuPharm (to pool expertise and ideas about potentially beneficial applications), and manufacturers like Honeywell are already leveraging quantum computing power within their organizations. In fact, the majority of "decision-makers plan to harness quantum computing in the near future," according to an ITProPortal September 2020 article and a 451 Research study.

So, what's driving this interest in quantum computing? Tangible returns. Faster development times. Greater efficiency.

Vastly greater amounts of data to cope with. Security of that data. The ability to address more complex problems that traditional computers cannot. The risk of falling behind the competition, some of which may not even exist yet. Many of the advantages of artificial intelligence in the last decade pose equal opportunities for quantum computing.

Is quantum computing a viable technology for organizations planning their future? According to Owen Rogers, Research Director at 451 Research, "the majority (81%) have use cases in mind for where quantum computing could make an impact". Quantum computing progressed in the last few years beyond merely academia or research labs and has been embraced by large organizations looking for financial returns and a competitive edge.

This relatively new and extremely complex technology has a big future and that's why this book is highly relevant today. Quantum Boost will inform decision-makers on what quantum computing is and its' advantages over traditional computing while being a proponent of continuing to use traditional computing as well. Being a disruptive technology, only now illustrating its potential, quantum computing is at an inflection point with significant barriers to cross yet a world of opportunity ahead.

While quantum computers are not expected to replace traditional computers completely, their use is manifold and expanding daily. Moore's Law, which predicted that the number of transistors in a dense integrated circuit (IC) doubles about every two years "will finally begin to degrade," predicts former Google CEO Eric Schmidt. Traditional computing may be reaching its computational limit just in time for quantum computing to emerge from the lab.

Rarely do we consider the transistor or integrated circuit today when using our laptop or desktop computers. The technology is decades old and we have come to trust, for the most part, the operating performance of the classical computer without understanding its inner workings. So, why write about the inner workings of a quantum computer? Exactly because it is new technology, yet to be trusted by most consumers because they have yet to gain confidence in the field or its participants.

Articles published online appear daily, reporting on some new discoveries related to quantum computing. If you seek to be a pioneer in computing, the time is now. If you aspire to be a fast follower/early adopter, the curve is accelerating and it becomes more likely follower and adopters will fall behind. Now is the time for a book to inform you, your decisions, and energize your organization. That's why I wrote Quantum Boost.

The overwhelming power of quantum computing is its superior capability to optimize and simulate complex problems. China recently announced a quantum device that performs 2.6 billion years of computation in 4 minutes using light photons to explore a quantum maze faster than any classical computer. But what sort of problems?

Allow me to share a practical problem that classic computing is challenged to answer, namely the traveling salesperson problem. Company A wants to send a salesperson from its head office to 14 separate cities in the optimal path. Today's best computers can perform that operation in seconds. Yet, increasing the number to 22 cities with the same laptop and algorithm could take 2,000 years.

Here is where quantum computing becomes invaluable since, for every additional city, the computing power required balloons. Really? Yes. For example, 11 cities translate to 20 million routes between them, 12 cities - 240 million routes and 15 cities - more than 650 billion. With every new city, the challenge becomes more extensive. If you are running an airline, add equipment readiness, passenger preferences, and numerous other factors to become an optimization nightmare. But not necessarily for a quantum computer.

According to CB Insights Tech Trends Report for 2020, "quantum tech is described as 'coming of age,' where advances in quantum computers and quantum cryptography will begin to stack up as more companies take notice of quantum tech's potential – with both excitement and a bit of apprehension."

Gartner completed a survey of 350+ CEO's from around the world about the shifting priorities of this role in 2021. The survey did ask respondents about quantum computing and the results may not be surprising. 69% of CEO's said they are don't know (13%) or feel quantum computing is not really a consideration to their long-range business plans (56%). It is those pioneering CEO's (31%) who state that "quantum computing progress is highly relevant to our long-range business plan".

Companies continue to struggle with finding value in quantum investments. The same 451 Research study completed in 2020 found that over a third of companies abandoned projects since 2017 given their complexity despite fully 97 percent believing that complex problem solving is either very important or critical. Unsurprisingly, quantum computing usage by business is evolving, with 39 percent of respondents saying they are experimenting and 81% say they have some use cases in mind for the next three years.

To illustrate quantum computing maturity, consider Gartner (the research and consulting firm) which produces their technology Hype Cycle Charts each year, identifying where each technology lies in terms of maturity level (5 stages). Not everything is rosy in the Gartner hype cycle, especially where most technologies fit in the "peak of inflated expectations." Since 2015, quantum computing has moved along the line from mere innovation to the peak of inflated expectations (every technology goes through these stages). Note: In 2020 Gartner moved Quantum Computing to the 'Hype Cycle for Compute Infrastructure', showing it at the 'Peak' level before 'sliding into the trough'. The graph promises a significant amount of activity in the next few years before quantum technology is considered mature. That is where quantum computing lies and Gartner has argued that quantum computing value is up to 10 years away. While others disagree, what a ride it should be.

Why am I arguing that it's so essential for organizations to act now? There are several reasons one needs to explore to believe in this new technology including its transformative potential, the pace of quantum progress, that in-house competency & culture takes time, and finally, quantum computing's steep learning curve.

Back in 2017, I had numerous conversations with companies about the transformational potential of AI. They were all valid. The same applies today to quantum computing. The transformative potential applies to value and supply chains in all industries and fields, particularly those with complex challenges to solve, like healthcare, research, finance, and chemistry, where traditional computers are less effective and complex sit on the shelf as a result. Organizations applying quantum computing will enable rapid gains in profitability and market share by solving problems competitors (and classical computers) cannot.

In a previous life, I was part of the leadership team of a transportation and distribution company. Attempting to optimize pick-up and delivery points for cargo was an incredible challenge, especially in an industry where margins were razor thin. Trying to satisfy numerous delivery system requirements, like Amazon during the holiday season, requires large scale logistics, artificial intelligence, and contemporary, traditional digital computers. Yet these computers operate in a linear fashion looking at one route at a time in sequence. Exploring every possibility could take millions of years, so probabilities are applied to a limited number of options. Based on current views, quantum computing could explore all possibilities simultaneously.

BCG principal Matt Langone at Q2B20 stated, "While classical computers are deterministic and operate serially — testing one possibility after another — quantum computers "operate probabilistically and simultaneously." Companies applying this technology could expand margins and improve customer service by truly optimizing routes faster.

As a banker in the early 21st century, we pursued a fast-follower approach to technology. While banks remain substantial entities today, we suffered from significant market losses by not pioneering as fintech companies did in capturing payments and credit offerings using artificial intelligence and swift delivery. Being a fast follower in the 2020s may not be enough as quantum computing appears in the business toolset. Quantum computing is characterized by a long-learning curve to understand where it should be applied, how 'noisy' they can be, how to find talent and partnerships to support the quantum campaign and so many more challenges this book will address. As in the case of AI, fast followers will be misnamed. In truth, these entities will be laggards overspending to try to catch up given the speed with which quantum computing competencies will supersede traditional computing. In some cases, it may be "winner-takes-all".

The 2020 study by 451 Research concluded there was significant momentum in entities exploring impactful quantum use cases for competitive advantage and not simply operational but financial benefit as well. As with AI, organizations trying to develop a quantum center of excellence (or even competence) will find that such a venture takes time. Considering that most business leaders have heard about quantum computing but have yet to act on the technology, competitive advantage is a very real probability for first movers.

As companies start to realize the potential impact of quantum technology, they will begin to invest in the technology at a rapid pace. Brian Burke, Chief of Research at Gartner told the Gartner

Symposium/ITxpo that 'By 2023, 20% of organisations will be budgeting for quantum computing projects compared to less than 1% today'. The challenge will be in whether their competition is ahead of them in the race, and they are able to align their technology strategy with their business objectives (much like what happened with artificial intelligence). The next few years will be a fascinating time for businesses that chase this technology imperative.

Cloud-based quantum computing is the dominant approach today in the commercial quantum ecosystem given the simpler nature of building fewer quantum computers and offering remote access to them through vendors like AWS and Microsoft Azure. Establishing trusted partnerships and vendor relationships and priority with organizations like these will be essential for pioneering firms.

Quantum resources are limited, growing to be sure with new educational offerings, but limited, nonetheless. During the last five years, the number of people transitioning into data science (DS) was explosive, with DS jobs being among the top 10 on LinkedIn and other lists. It will take some time before that phenomenon exists for quantum computing, so the talent pool for the 'center' may take an extended period to collect at a premium price in a competitive QC era.

Even when your organization has onboarded such talent, creating a cohesive, transformational group will be challenging. Ensuring senior leadership championing of investment, and culture transformation is but one critical task. Embracing new partnerships with QC vendors, shifting priorities, updating training programs, and not relying solely on external parties to drive your QC strategy.

Given the transformative nature of QC and the time to build out an internal QC competency, the time to act is, indeed, now. So, invest time in reading Quantum Boost to accelerate and supercharge your business.

Chapter 2

What is Quantum Computing?

"If quantum mechanics hasn't profoundly shocked you, you haven't understood it yet" – Niels Bohr (20th Century Danish Physicist on Atomic and Quantum Theory)

In my experience with the evolution of Artificial Intelligence, business leaders tried to implement AI as any other technology and the majority of projects failed. The black box, job insecurity, bias, people challenges and hype were all part of the AI reality. Quantum computing (QC) is maturing even faster than AI (the speed at which quantum breakthroughs are taking place), so business leaders need to be prepared today for this complex technology.

According to an ITProPortal September article and the 451 Research study the majority of "decision-makers plan to harness quantum computing in the near future." There could be between 2,000 and 5,000 quantum computers worldwide by 2030 and $1 trillion in global market value according to McKinsey & Co.

'Quantum computing' phrase searches have moved little over the past 5 years, yet in the last 12 months, searches for 'quantum computing stocks' have risen 500%, for 'bitcoin quantum computing' 250% and 'quantum computing companies' 180%. In terms of media coverage, quantum computing saw a 64% increase in 2020. Headlines proliferate such as "Google's supremacy," "progress in IBM's quantum volume"; "leaps in D-Wave Advantage qubits to 5,000"; "China's photonic advances,"; and "Cambridge Quantum Computing (UK) receives the largest funding for a software firm." Every day there is a new development in quantum computing.

So, what's driving this interest in quantum computing? Tangible returns. Faster development times. Greater efficiency. The ability to address more complex problems that traditional computers cannot. The risk of falling behind the competition, some of which may not even exist yet. Many of the advantages of artificial intelligence in the last decade pose equal opportunities for quantum computing.

The first quantum revolution introduced nuclear power, imaging devices, lasers, MRI's, and new rules that govern physical reality. First labelled by Jonathan Dowling and Gerard Milburn in a 2003 paper the "2nd Quantum Revolution", we are entering the so-called 'second quantum revolution' (SQR) where engineering of quantum solutions occur that originated from the first quantum revolution. The SQR (refers to the manipulation and control of atoms, ions, photons, electrons, even molecules) reaching the limit of measurement accuracy at quantum levels) is a massive step forward toward the commercialization of quantum technologies as you will observe throughout the remainder of this book.

What about the barriers to adopting this new technology? In February 2021 an online survey conducted by the Quantum Computing Summit and Omdia found that not only were few companies surveyed (2%) stated they "have a live deployment of QC across at least one business function." Why would that be the case? Four reasons rose to the top, which were as familiar in the early days of AI as they are now for quantum computing. The four reasons from the survey include:

- A lack of knowledge about QC and its possibilities among respondents
- A relatively limited level of engagement with other stakeholders, including partnerships between end-users and providers
- Limited in-house expertise, expertise, or skills relating to QC
- No budget, limited budgets, or uncertain budgets for QC

These reasons, in particular the knowledge aspect of QC, is the reason I wrote 'Quantum Boost'. To not just explain what quantum computing is, but how it can benefit organizations as well with practical examples. Is quantum computing a viable technology for organizations planning their future? According to Owen Rogers, Research Director at 451 Research, "the majority (81%) have use cases in mind for where quantum computing could make an impact". Quantum computing has progressed in the last few years beyond academia or research labs and has been embraced by large organizations looking for financial returns and a competitive edge.

I'm not alone in the belief that quantum computing will have a significant impact on the business world and sooner rather than later. Alan Baratz, CEO of Canada's D-Wave Systems Inc., said in 2019 that he "joined D-Wave to bring technology to the enterprise. Now more than ever, I am convinced that making practical quantum computing available to forward-thinking businesses and emerging quantum developers through the cloud is central to jumpstarting the broad development of in-production quantum applications." Yaoyun Shi, head of China-based Alibaba's Quantum Laboratory says "…I really put emphasis on the end applications—I want to see our customers benefiting from our quantum technology.'" With the deep pockets of Alibaba, Shi and company can make that happen.

Before going public in 2021, IonQ's CEO Peter Chapman articulated his company's focus on the hardware niche of ion trap quantum computers. He said in 2019, "We at IonQ are just focused on producing the world's best quantum computer." Honeywell, another corporate monolith agreed by focusing on the same quantum technology, ion trap. The relatively newcomer manufacturer, Rigetti Computing, founded just 8 years ago by former IBM Quantum Lab employee Dave Rigetti, focuses on the full quantum stack. Rigetti is an entrepreneur as well as an applied physicist, saying he wanted to "to build a company from the ground up to really solve the essential problems that need to be solved to make QC truly useful for the world."

Venture capital (VC) has been a major source of quantum technology funding in its early stages of maturity, especially in North America. With so many hardware manufacturers and types of quantum technology (we discuss eight in a later chapter), there may be a weeding out in the future, with venture capital being directed to eventual winners. With a public share price to track in IonQ, VC's are better positioned to consider exit prices for their investments. While large organizations like Intel are actively developing more powerful chips, including the quantum variety, commercial viability will be a driving target for manufacturers,

While quantum computers are not expected to replace traditional computers completely, their use is manifold and expanding daily. Moore's Law, which predicted that the number of transistors in a dense integrated circuit (IC) doubles about every two years, "will finally begin to degrade," predicts former Google CEO Eric Schmidt. Traditional computing may be reaching its computational limit just in time for quantum computing to emerge from the lab.

Quantum computing is not just for decision-makers in the largest of organizations. Within a few years, quantum computing will be more relevant for smaller-sized companies seeking to solve similar complex problems. This relatively new and extremely complex technology has a big future and that's why this book is highly relevant today. Quantum Boost will inform decision-makers on what quantum computing is and its' advantages over traditional computing while being a proponent of continuing to use traditional computing as well. Being a disruptive technology, only now illustrating its potential, quantum computing is at an inflection point with significant barriers to cross yet a world of opportunity ahead.

If you picked up this book to learn about quantum computing for business, you're in the right place. If you hoped to gain the latest insights in quantum math, physics and mechanics at their deepest levels, there are better sources available. If you're interested in learning about the commercial possibilities originating from the smallest scale elements that humans are aware of, then, again, you're in the right place. Let's get started.

Explaining Quantum Computing

Quantum computing, while exotic sounding and based in mechanics that should 'profoundly shock you' as Niels Bohr said almost 100 years ago, can be understood at levels useful to business leaders. In essence, this century we will use the ultra-small, quantum properties of material to process information. Linking these phenomena to computation is part of that process.

Let's take our first example. A robot stands at the entrance to a maze. In traditional computing, the robot will be instructed to take a step, assess where there is an open space in front of it or a barrier stopping it from moving forward. The robot performs this activity in a linear sequence. One step forward. Assess. Make the next move. Until the robot finds the sequence of steps to get to the maze exit.

Now we apply the capabilities of a quantum computer. There are an infinite number of robots at the entrance. Each takes a different path simultaneously. In the time it's taking the traditional computer to assess a single path, a quantum computer is considering all paths. One of the QC robots will find the correct path much faster than the single robot looking at one path at a time. Much like the city example we learned about in the "Why This Book and Why Now" section.

Consider the challenges an airline encounters every day. Which passengers on which planes to which cities at which time accommodating which changes under which airport and weather constraints? For every new factor the complexity of scheduling becomes ever more difficult to optimize. Not so for a quantum computer. What would take hundreds or thousands of years for an airline to discover the optimal schedule every day may be accomplished in a fraction of the time with a quantum computer. Rather than oversell or hype quantum computing's power, I will describe the challenges for today's era of QC so that readers have a clear sense of the technology's maturity and predictions for error-free or error-corrected fault tolerant (resistant against errors) quantum computing in the future.

One of the key powers of any current day computer is to create simulations. Virtual representations of physical assets or processes are possible in varying levels of sophistication as in the case of digital twins (creating virtual representations of physical assets like jet engines, buildings or factories). Yet traditional computers must follow a linear path. Researching molecule combinations to create something new takes a great deal of time even with artificial intelligence. Applying quantum computation to simulation trials allows the user to attempt numerous simultaneous tests in virtual space. Hopefully this potential has you mentally revisiting the top strategies for your upcoming year.

Quantum computing (QC) is a new (think the past decade) way of computing. Rather than using the classical bit paradigm (1's and 0's, on or off states), quantum computers use something called qubits. Qubits can have two states, 1 and 0 at the same time. The advantage of a qubit over a bit is the number of states it can represent and the exponential increment in capacity of information it can hold. Also quantum computers take advantage of this entangling of the states to compute in parallel all possible states versus the linear, one state at a time computation of a classical computer, thus in highly specific cases today, achieve computation exponentially speedier than their classical counterparts.

Some believe like Paul Smith-Goodson, a quantum computing analyst with Moor Insights & Strategy, that "it will take millions of qubits to be able to complete calculations that have meaningful results for businesses, so the industry is still a few years away from achieving the quantum advantage. "

Several companies have taken the lead in developing quantum computers, namely Honeywell (as of writing, the fastest quantum computer at 64 qubits), as well as DWave, IBM and Righetti. These companies, much like those manufacturers of the original personal computers and their chips, are racing for supremacy in the fastest, least error, most cost-effective quantum computers.

How Quantum Computing Works

Gonzalo Florez Giraldo, founder and CEO at Quantum Computing Engineering, Inc offered a straightforward description of quantum computing. " Quantum computing is a radically new way to store and process information based on the principles of quantum mechanics. While conventional computers store information in binary "bits" that are either 0s or 1s, quantum computers store information in quantum bits, or qubits.

A qubit can be both 0 and 1 at the same time, and a series of qubits together remember many different things simultaneously.

Scott Adams' Dilbert on Quantum:
Boss: How's your quantum computer prototype coming along?
Wally: Great!
Wally: The project exists in a simultaneous state of being both totally successful and not even started.
Boss: Can I observe it?
Wally: That's a tricky question?

Quantum technology attempts to harness the unique properties of our smallest scale elements, atoms, electrons and photons to process computations more efficiently than a traditional computer. These properties are superposition, wave nature, and entanglement. Photons, for example, exhibiting a quantum state called entanglement permits these photons to share information over great distances without a physical connection.

Several companies have taken the lead in developing quantum computers, namely Honeywell (as of writing, the fastest quantum computer at 64 qubits), as well as DWave, IBM and Righetti. These companies, much like those manufacturers the original personal computers and their chips, are racing for supremacy in the fastest, lest error, most cost-effective quantum computers.

Certainly, arguments occur in the press and academia that predicting the rate of future quantum computing maturity is speculative at best. Improving the number of qubits, reducing error rates for storage and operations, and enhancing quantum programming languages are tall orders yet the rate of acceleration in 2020 has been exciting.

Development of qubit devices operating at a very cold 1.5 Kelvin (UNSW Sydney), noise cancelling for quantum bits through ML reducing noise to 0% in a quantum chip (multiple universities), the control of single atoms in electronic devices and Honeywell's development of a 64-qubit device has all occurred in the first half of 2020. D-Wave, the Canadian entity now reports a quantum programming community of over 1,000 developers applying QC to financial modeling, transportation routes, and protein folding. Its Leap2 system supports up to 10,000 variables, which can be fully connected with one another.

Entanglement

Imagine being at a fast-food restaurant ordering takeout. You decide to order a hamburger and a hot dog. Once cooked, they are given to you in two identical boxes. You don't know which box has the hamburger and which holds the hot dog. Once you open one box, say the hamburger box, then you know with reasonable certainty that the other holds the hot dog. In this way the two boxes are entangled. If one is a hamburger, then the other must be a hotdog. This analogy roughly describes quantum entanglement.

We said earlier that quantum refers to the smallest elements we know of namely photons (particles that make up light), and protons, electrons and neutrons (the particles that comprise an atom). In terms of size, billions of electrons could fit on the tip of a needle.

When a pair of particles are generated in such a way that the state of one particle cannot be described independently of the state of the others, regardless of the distance separating them, they are quantum entangled. Particles can also be entangled by their spin and polarization which will be covered later in this chapter. Without being able to fully explain this phenomenon, Einstein called it "spooky action at a distance". Regardless, entanglement allows us to use quantum circuits to manipulate data from the real world given correlations between it and a quantum system.

In the case of quantum entanglement, let's consider two electrons. First, we must find the electrons by plotting them. So how do quantum physicists identify where the electrons are? If one were to a plot a coordinate of some object on earth they would use latitude, longitude, and height (3 dimensions) to identify its location. Sometimes this is represented by an x, y and z axis. Even done to the smallest size, no two objects can have the same x,y,z coordinates (ie occupy the same space). Adding a fourth dimension of time (t - where the object was located at a certain time), then no two objects can have the same four coordinates (x,y,z, and t).

So too with the infinitely small particles like electrons. An electron has four quantum numbers, namely n, l, m(l) and m(s). More specifically they are:

n = principal quantum number
l = orbital angular momentum quantum number
m(l) = magnetic quantum number
m(s) = electron spin quantum number

When we consider m(s) or electron spin quantum number, spin is defined as the intrinsic value of the angular momentum of a fundamental particle. An electron can have either a positive spin (spin up) or a negative spin (spin down) value.

Now this is where quantum mechanics gets a little less obvious, straightforward...actually just plain weird. The electron is not necessarily spinning as it can exist in both states at once which is called superposition. We'll come back to that topic next.

The way a quantum computer links two qubits (particles mentioned earlier like photons) together occurs by entering specific commands in the computer entangling them. If something happens to one qubit, instantaneously its mate reacts. Combining many networks such qubits, numerous parallel operations can occur at once, thus quantum computing's exponential capability.

To make this phenomenon even more interesting, the distance between the two qubits doesn't affect their entanglement. They can be miles or even light years apart and remain entangled. The qubits will continue to act in strongly correlated ways which permits quantum computers to take advantage of that interdependence.

Once two electrons are entangled, they can only have opposite spins. In their natural state they have both up and down spin simultaneously. If one electron is measured to have up spin, then the second immediately becomes down spin. Entangled particles behave together as a system, so linking quantum computers can illustrate information about physical properties of the system.

So, what would some practical benefits of quantum entanglement be? Consider the clock. Clocks around the world often lose or gain time. The atomic clock is the most accurate clock we have yet it is not used by everyone. A quantum logic clock will neither lose nor gain a second in 33 billion years. Regardless of distance or other factors. Having consistent accuracy through quantum clocks for world stock exchanges (trading in nanoseconds) and GPS systems would be hugely beneficial. Randomly polarized photons being entangled with each other to provide quantum cryptography – quantum key distribution is used today to create highly secure networks – where any changes to the photon's quantum states would be identified.

Superposition Explained

A coin is at rest on a table. The face of the coin is either a head or a tail. One state or the other. Now place the coin on its edge and spin it quickly. Which state is the coin in? Neither heads nor tails? Or both at the same time?

Now, cover the head face with a "0" and the tail face with a "1". If the head face is showing on the coin sitting flat on the table, then you know the state is "0". Place the coin on its edge again and spin it quickly. Is the state a "0" or a "1"? It is both simultaneously. This is the concept of superposition.

In traditional computing a bit can be a "0" or "1" but not both. The bit can be one state only, either "on" or "off". In quantum computing, quantum bits or qubits (those particles referred to earlier) can assume any combination of gradations between zero and one. So, what does superposition then offer to computing? It allows qubits to store incredible amounts of data as compared to traditional bits. In fact, a quantum computer with n qubits can have all 2n possibilities in superposition with one another giving them an exponential group of states to explore in problem solving. Electrons also exist in a natural state of superposition of both up and down spin. Only when measured can you define which it is at that point in time.

Noise & Errors

Organizational leaders, in my personal experience over 30 years of corporate and SME involvement, need to be convinced of a new technologies' stability, accuracy, speed and reliability before investing and placing their clients or brand at risk. An enormous amount of progress has been made over the last five decades in the field of quantum computing. Yet, since the early days of quantum research, quantum noise's contribution to computing error meant exposure to such risks and constructed investment barriers.

Today we are in the era of "noisy intermediate-scale quantum" or NISQ computers. What does this mean? Well, so-called noisy qubits may return biased and/or erroneous results for early quantum algorithm applications. In fact, according to Joel

Wallman, a researcher at the Institute for Quantum Computing (IQC) and assistant professor of applied mathematics at the University of Waterloo, "The intrinsic noise in quantum computers makes their output unreliable." As John Preskill, an American theoretical physicist known for coining the term "quantum supremacy" noted, "noise in quantum gates will limit the size of quantum circuits that can be executed reliably."

Researchers will continue in this noisy era to pursue something referred to as "fault tolerance". The lack of reliability from qubit decoherence (any partial collapse of the quantum information associated with the qubit) and the resulting performance challenges would, in theory, disappear with the fault tolerant quantum computer. A computer that operates at extremely low levels of noise.

How will the quantum computing industry know when it has achieved fault tolerance? That answer is based in the quantum threshold theorem which states if a quantum computer has a large qubit count (over 10,000) and can limit noise to under 1%, it has met the threshold. Essentially correcting errors faster than they occur through massive number of qubits (many believe that number to 1 million).

Optical communications often use amplitude modulation. In the case of lasers, electrical field amplitude and phase can contribute to quantum noise. Quantum noise refers to the "uncertainty of a physical quantity that is due to its quantum origin or said differently the error of the description of any physical system within classical (not quantum) theory". Industrial noise, vibrations, gases, voltage fluctuations and thermal disturbances being experienced/suppressed can impact quantum computer accuracy.

One such quantum computing challenge occurs with readout errors which traditionally arise from either measurement times being significant in relation to qubit decoherence times (where the state decays during measurement) or a small probability of measuring the opposite qubit value. Researchers like Nachman et al continue to investigate a "potential tool for correcting readout errors from universal gate-based quantum computers."

Two Australian University of Sydney students have provided hope for improved error corrections. Bonilla and Brown's "new code doubles the error suppression compared with previous error correction code" by rotating the coordinates on every other qubit in the system. The discovery now moves to Amazon Web Services (AWS) which is now part of the collaboration along with scientists at Yale University. Estimates of the universal fault tolerant quantum computer being decades away are being challenged with daily quantum discoveries.

Quantum Speed & Hybrid Solvers

One of the key outcomes of the Multiverse – D-Wave effort is the quantum computer performed that analysis in only 171 seconds or 2.85 minutes. Using a classical computing approach with Tensor Networks to achieve the same results…it took over 32 hours of processing time. But this is just a model you say. No. D-Wave's hybrid solver service run on its quantum processor with Multiverse Computing's algorithm recently performed this breakthrough with real historical data.

The quantum ecosystem should not be driven solely by its technology. The world is composed of mostly classical computing technology, and not every problem requires the power of a quantum computer. Where the magic happens is when solvers are both classical and quantum – otherwise termed hybrid. The concept behind a hybrid solver service is the coordination of work between the CPU and the quantum computer using that framework to optimize a hybrid workflow.

Determining the mix or ratio of CPU and QPU to apply depends on the problem being solved. Fortunately the two systems are complementary towards most applications or use cases, and leveraging the strengths of each renders the optimal hybrid-solver solution.

Business leaders of the current generation must recognize that classical computing solutions will not be expiring or becoming extinct anytime soon. So, deriving the optimal technology investment means working with providers that recognize the beauty of hybrid capabilities and when to apply them to your goals. Businesses can leverage classical computation on its own, as a comparator to quantum computing for reasonableness checks on accuracy, or when the problem is too complex for a classical computer, offer the only vehicle to a solution through quantum. Yet extracting the strengths from both solutions will drive significant benefits for today's organization.

Are We Making Progress in 2021?

Wallman is also the co-founder of IQC startup Quantum Benchmark. He and other colleagues recently improved upon previous error assessment protocols which were only effective in detecting errors on a small subset of the qubits. Detecting error correlations and providing an estimate of the effective noise within arbitrary sets of qubits offers greater accuracy potential based on their new method.

Cambridge Quantum Computing announced in 2020 a collaboration with CERN to "to explore the application of quantum technologies to particle physics" with a view to "help the members of the CERN openlab project team to work across multiple platforms to achieve optimal results even on today's noisy quantum hardware."

In more macro terms, Cape Town, South Africa hosted the upcoming ICQNI 2021: 15 or International Conference on Quantum Noise and Information on April 22–23, 2021. The conference brings together a diverse group of scholarly events (geared towards industry researchers, academics, and students) allowing participants to exchange ideas, trends and issues related to the field of quantum noise. It is from conferences like these where leading voices can progress the effort to hush such noise. According to ICQNI, “the peer-reviewed conference proceedings are indexed in the Open Science Index, Google Scholar, Semantic Scholar, Zenedo, OpenAIRE, BASE, WorldCAT, Sherpa/RoMEO, and other index databases.”

Being able to produce quantum chips on an industrial scale has been a driving factor in predictions about scalable quantum computing being decades away. In 2021, Quantum Motion, a UK-based company building a scalable array of qubits fabricated on silicon, announced a major breakthrough towards industrial, scalable production of quantum computing chips. According to The Quantum Daily, "Quantum Motion has been able to demonstrate state-of-the-art quantum capabilities using industrial-grade silicon chips, helping to set a blueprint for how quantum chips can be manufactured at scale using existing manufacturing processes. The discovery has been peer reviewed in the scientific journal PRX Quantum." What this means according to the London-based company, is that it is "possible to create a stable qubit on a standard silicon chip" (for nine seconds they isolated and measured the quantum state of a single electron on a CMOS or Complementary Metal–Oxide–Semiconductor, chip), rather than solely in a lab environment. It will be interesting to see if this technology breakthrough leads to a commoditization of quantum computers.

Another barrier to scalability is wiring where manufacturers need to increase the density of signaling and wiring to handle the qubit traffic absent degrading the stability of the system. Add to this stability challenges when considering the vulnerability of qubits to fluctuations from noise as discussed earlier in this chapter. Maintaining a qubit in a coherent state in the early days of quantum computing occurred over a period of nanoseconds which made it difficult to drive any activities in such a short period of time. More recently through cooling at cryogenic temperatures, coherence could be maintained for up to 100 seconds which would permit a thousand information processing operations before the coherence was lost. One group based in Japan, the RIKEN Superconducting Quantum Electronics Research Team (along with other institutes) developed a new circuit wiring scheme to create larger, more effective quantum circuits with expectations to scale up to 100+ qubits within the decade.

Measuring Progress

While many are pursuing the challenge of hushing noisy qubits (or more accurately the noise that is impacting qubits), others are attempting to measure the progress. IBM (which manufactures superconducting quantum computers) suggests that "quantum volume" is a more accurate measure of quantum computing capability than merely the number of qubits as it incorporates the "measure of the circuits' quality; the higher the quality, the more complex circuits can be run on a quantum computer" in this case "2 to the power of the size of the largest circuit with equal width and depth that can pass a certain reliability test involving random two-qubit gates."

IonQ, a global leader in trapped ion quantum computers, argues that 'algorithmic qubits' are a better measure than either straight qubits or qubit volume. They even provide an algorithmic qubit calculator on their website which factors in physical qubits, average 2Q fidelity, and error correction overhead.

D-Wave's VP of Product Management, Murray Thom, says "instead of devoting most of our team's resources to determining how we build quantum systems, we are now more focused on exploring how we continue to improve the performance and scale of our systems so that businesses can benefit."

If you're a student of quantum computing progress, you'll see dozens of media articles talking about the number of qubits from tens to thousands, yet what really matters is the usable qubit, and the ability to leverage accurate computations from this new technology. Businesses want tools that progress their strategies and have a positive business impact. They are not pursuing the perfect technology. The future is bright for quantum computing but in 2021, there's still lots of work to do, and in the meantime, business can leverage incremental impact.

Chapter 3

The Quantum Technology Stack & Wars

"We're not trying to meet some flashy goal. We're trying to build that rocket to the moon.

Jim Clarke, Head of Quantum Hardware, Intel

Quantum computing represents the fifth generation of computers. First-generation computers began in the 1940s with vacuum tubes. Then around 1956, transistors emerged, followed by integrated circuits in about 1964, and the fourth generation was microprocessors starting in 1971. (For this book, we will refer to earlier generations as 'classical computers').

So, what's the fifth generation? The World Economic Forum's "Global Future Council on Quantum Computing" states, "quantum computers can do computation differently and with exponentially greater power. They are not just accelerated versions of classical computers; they are fundamentally different."

Organizations considering quantum computing as an opportunity need to think about where within the quantum tech stack they will "play". Each organization must select where their core capabilities exist and where it would be more cost-effective or efficient to invest their efforts, keeping in mind the relative immaturity of the quantum computing field.

Doug Finke, managing editor of the Quantum Computing Report, shared an excellent visual of the quantum tech stack at a recent London gathering, the contents of which create the foundation for any buy, borrow, build decision.

At the bottom or foundation of the tech stack is the **quantum chip,** also referred to as quantum processor or QPU (quantum processing unit). According to Science Alert, QPU's "perform calculations based on the probability of an object's state before it is measured — instead of just 1s or 0s — which means they have the potential to process exponentially more data compared to classical computers".

Quantum computer manufacturers, namely Honeywell, D-Wave, IBM and Rigetti much like those manufacturers of the original personal computers and their chips, are racing for supremacy in the fastest, lest error, most cost-effective quantum computers. Circuit-based QPU's include IBM's superconducting chips which have held such names as Armonk, Ourense, Vigo, London, Burlington, Essex, etc. Annealing QPU's include D-Wave's series (2X, 2000Q, Advantage). Photonic or light-based architecture includes Xanadu's X8, X12, X24. Honeywell and IonQ produce ion trap QPU's. Released over time, each processor varies in fidelity, speed and qubit capacity.

Full stack technology vendors do exist and The Quantum Daily considers a Canadian firm like Xanadu as one to watch. Founded in 2016, the company provides both software and hardware and cloud services based on quantum photonic semiconductors. To boot, they offer a host of Beatles nomenclature products including Penny Lane (ML platform for quantum computers), Strawberry Fields (full stack Python library) and Blackbird (quantum programming language)

Indeed, arguments occur in the press and academia that predicting the rate of future quantum computing maturity is speculative at best. Improving the number of qubits, reducing error rates for storage and operations, and enhancing quantum programming languages are tall orders, yet the rate of acceleration in 2020 has been exciting.

Transpilers come next in the stack. Amelie Schreiber, writer in *Towards Data Science*, describes transpilers as source-to-source compilers which "take one version of code, optimize it in some way, perhaps by shortening the code, reducing the amount of memory needed to run the code, or reducing the runtime of the code, and the new optimized is the output of the transpiler." Qiskit, IBM's open-source framework for quantum computing, defines transpilation as "the process of rewriting a given input circuit to match the topoplogy of a specific quantum device, and/or to optimize the circuit for execution on present day noisy quantum systems."

Control electronics firmware is the next highest level, being either a standard operating environment for more complex device software or as a complete OS (control, monitoring, data manipulation) for less sophisticated devices. Companies like Q-CTRL provide "a set of protocols that connect quantum hardware with higher, more abstract levels in the quantum computing stack... to bridge the divide between quantum algorithms and imperfect hardware".

The **software framework** rests above the transpiler and firmware providing generic, reusable functionality which can be changed through additional user-written code, translating into software that is application specific. Specific examples include code libraries, compilers, and API's (application programming interface) that bring components together. Quantum Machines of Israel, for example, promotes its Quantum Orchestration Platform for "any company or institution developing quantum processors...can now purchase the QOP to run the most complex algorithms possible”. Their software interface/quantum assembler (QUA) translates classical code “into a quantum assembler language that can then be run on any quantum processor.”

Software routine libraries are “debugged blocks of code (subroutine, procedure, function etc.), often designed to handle commonly occurring problems or tasks”
per ComputerScience.GCSE.GURU Quantum software libraries include IBM’s Qiskit, Microsoft’s Quantum Development Kit Chemistry Library, TensorFlow’s and Baidu Paddle QML versions.

Cloud infrastructure, by no means a new technology, incorporates the components required for cloud computing such as hardware, storage, and networking enabling hosting services.

Education and User Communities, like those offered by quantumcomputing.com, IEEE, IBM, Waterloo’s Institute for Quantum Computing, Atos, and others bring together customers and users of various quantum ecosystems. Such communities encourage users to share their experiences, reviews and insights independent of quantum vendors or suppliers.

As someone new to quantum technology, read the rest of this book before making decisions about your own organization’s quantum investment strategy to ensure you have considered all the relevant factors in those decisions. Not to mention, there are numerous types of quantum computers which are discussed in the next section.

The Quantum Computing Wars

As of writing there are at least eight different leading types of quantum computer technology. So, if you're a decision-maker which path to choose? In this section, we'll explore these eight subtypes, the applications, and the big players in each type. Note to reader: There is no one dominant universal quantum computer type today, and each has its own strengths, weaknesses and use case application.

Annealing/Adiabatic:

In the pursuit of making a material more ductile, softer and more workable annealing is the process of heating that material to alter its physical and chemical properties. The process requires the material to be heated beyond its recrystallization temperature followed by cooling. Quantum annealing (QA) is employed by some quantum hardware manufacturers to identify over a set of candidates states the global minimum of an objective function (i.e. lowest energy level, size, distance). Quantum annealing appears to be best used where there is a discrete search space such as optimization problems like the traveling salesman problem. D-Wave is one of the most well-known quantum annealing companies along with Japanese company NEC Corporation.

The D-Wave Quantum Experience

While touring labs and museums these days is impossible in-person due to the pandemic, I've enjoyed virtual walkthroughs instead. One in particular caught my attention, that being D-Wave's quantum computing lab and museum. Yes, a company only 20 years old has a museum, this one located in Burnaby, BC, Canada. If you're starting to learn about quantum computer hardware, this is a great introduction from a company that focuses on the practical application of this advanced technology.

The tours are available to YouTube users. They're broken up into 4 parts (as of today) with descriptions of previous generations of chips, sample holders, control electronics, wafers, fabrication masks, unit cells, couplers...I could go on. The museum maintains a Patent Wall (at least until they ran out of room - they're over 160 now), and a Poster Wall which explains the history of D-Wave Systems and its processors.

Yet the most interesting part of the tour for me was getting to the 'dilution fridge' or refrigerator. If you've cozied up to quantum computing articles, posts, or white papers in the past few years, like I have, you've heard about noise, errors, and interference all of which impact the pure processing and accuracy of quantum processors. A walkthrough of the D-Wave Advantage hardware illustrates how the various shield levels address those issues.

In the simplest terms, deep cold removes noise, hard vacuums remove gases, and Farraday cages remove electromagnetic disturbances. In terms of noise protection, D-Wave's quantum chip operates in an environment of 15 milliKelvins or less above absolute zero at the bottom of the 'chandelier' with several stages above that reducing the temperature from 50 Kelvins (K) to 3K to 1 K and so on. Shielding in the form of a 'vacuum can' operates around the system to eliminate external gases/gas molecules from the dilution fridge/chamber. Electromagnetic interference or disturbances are eliminated by a Farraday cage.

Knowing how a quantum computer operates, especially within such a clean environment is helpful. Yet has the technology reached a practical level for businesses? The D-Wave client list, including Lockheed Martin (their original client), Google, NASA Ames, Volkswagen, DENSO, USRA, USC, Los Alamos National Laboratory, and Oak Ridge National Laboratory would say so.

Initiatives by companies like D-Wave Systems supported Covid research by offering free time on their systems. Certainly, quantum companies have the ability to address such laudable objectives like those embedded in the UN Sustainability Goals. The potential for quantum computing systems to address traffic flow, ocean clean-up, medical research, education, clean energy and so much more is near.

Who knows what the D-Wave Systems' Museum will look like in a few years? Maybe a few more walls will be required to house the many advancements in quantum computing hardware.

Superconducting:

When one thinks of quantum computing in its current day, most global enthusiasts think of IBM. Since 2016, IBM has strived for the lead in the new field and has focused on superconducting technology. The set of physical properties in materials known as superconductivity occurs in the disappearance of electrical resistance and dispelling of magnetic flux fields. Where typical metallic conductors resistance decreases over time as temperature is lowered to near absolute zero, superconductors have critical temperatures when resistance drops quickly to zero. Propelling an electric current through a superconducting wire loop, for example, can continue essentially indefinitely. In terms of a superconducting quantum computer, manufacturers like Google, IBM, IMEC, BBN Technologies, Rigetti, and Intel implement superconducting electronic circuits.

Trapped Ion

Quantum computers based on trapped ion technology leverages the properties of charged atomic particles called ions which can be suspended using electromagnetic fields. In this case, stable electronic states are created to store qubits for information processing. Quantum information transfers through the ions quantized motion in a shared trap while lasers induce coupling between qubits states. Some research suggests a high degree of accuracy using ion trap technology and a strong candidate for scalability, while others suggest the processing speed falls short of other technologies (though quantum inherently remains faster than classical computing for complex computational problems in general). Manufacturers include Honeywell International Inc., and IonQ .

Cold/Neutral/Helium Atoms:

Unlike ion-based quantum processing, neutral atoms have a physical property where they are easily held in close confinement with each other. One entity, The Anderson Group, along with eight other institutions, leverages Cesium atoms in a 2D array and a theoretical maximum lifetime of 100 seconds. Atom loss is monitored and reloaded as necessary within the array within the world's first neutral atom quantum computer.

Quantum Dots:

Capable of transporting electrons, quantum dots are crystals of nanoscale that are man-made and have optical and electronic properties. Artificial semiconducting nanoparticles react when UV light hits them (photoluminescence), exciting the electrons inside the quantum dot and emitting a diversity of colors which correlates to certain energy levels. QustomDot, a Ghent, Belgium-based QD technology company founded in 2020, operates on "non-restricted cadmium-free QDs, stable enough for on-chip usage."

Does the quantum dot market have scale? While a limiting factor may be the availability of rare earth materials, the overall global market is forecast to grow to US 10 billion by 2025 from 3.5 billion today. Where have quantum dots vendors like Samsung Electronics, Nanosys, Nanoco Group & QD Laser identified applications? In fluorescent biological labels, solar cells and composites. Applications include LED and LCD lighting displays, and mini and micro LED's. Nano-Lit Technologies, a company focused on lighting for health and well-being, uses quantum dots and advanced manufacturing to produce high quality, which emulates the sun's colour temperature shift, and restores circadian rhythms among other benefits.

Nitrogen Vacancy Diamonds:

You knew that diamonds had to enter into the quantum computing conversation somewhere. They do. One of the defects in a diamond is the nitrogen-vacancy center or NVC. Once again, the physical property is photoluminescence intensity. The NVC's electron spin can be manipulated much like other quantum technologies do through magnetics, microwave radiation, and electric fields of light. One of the major benefits of nitrogen vacancy diamonds (NVD) is its ability to operate at room temperatures (think no large refrigerators to cool atoms and slow their spin) at room temperature which is a significant benefit. The NVC becomes the basic unit for the quantum computer, or qubit with applications in sensor technology, cryptography and novel electronics.

Photonics:

Developed from 1960's work on semiconductor light emitters and optical fiber 10 years later, photonic quantum computers use the element photons (or light) which provide a higher bandwidth than electrons in conventional computers. Photonics covers the detection, generation and manipulation of light through a series of activities including amplifying, sensing, modulating, transmitting and generating photons. Photonic quantum computer manufacturers include AegiQ (UK), Cambridge Quantum Computing (UK), Hamamatsu Photonics (Japan), iPronics (Spain), Miraex (Switzerland), M Squared (UK), Nordic Quantum Computing Group (Norway), Nu Quantum (UK)

Topological:

Microsoft has been pursuing a topological quantum computer solution for many years based on anyons ("elementary particle or particle-like excitation having properties intermediate between those of bosons and fermions)." The anyon is called a Majorana fermion or Majorana bound state. The theory is that Majorana bound states allows them to be used as a building block for a topological quantum computer. To date no group has been able to prompt electrons into forming a Majorana particle. In fact, Microsoft affiliated researchers in March 2021 retracted a 2018 Nature article which formed the basis of their research.

Quantum Analog

infinityQ, the self-titled "quantum-analog device innovator" based in Montreal, Canada, has taken yet a different path to quantum computing in the form of an analog quantum computer toward optimization solving, and other challenges at room temperature over the cloud. infinitityQ's system, called inifinityQube, which leverages existing chip technologies promises less energy consumption aligning with edge computing needs. The technology has yet to be launched as of writing but offers an intriguing model for quantum of the future.

Digital Annealing

This book would be incomplete without addressing some quantum-inspired technology like Fujitsu's Digital Annealer. Sitting between classical computing and pure quantum computing plays, the digital annealer technology solution leverages inspiration from quantum elements such as superposition and entanglement to compute, in parallel, numerous potential options and provide accelerated insights.

Operating at room temperature over digital circuits, the digital annealer can address problems classical computers cannot by permitting the free exchange of signals across all bits (8,192-bit connectivity; 64-bit (2^{64}) gradations) not requiring programming rather setting parameters allows calculations to be performed, according to Fujitsu. Digital annealing, while not promising quantum annealing speed, promises stability (through a room temperature state) that qubits cannot offer currently.

There are numerous varieties of quantum computers out there, as described above, which can be confusing for business decision makers hoping to take advantage of the relatively new tech. When we see an example of convergence, it's an exciting proposition. As I mentioned earlier, in the search for a universal quantum computer, there is yet to be a standard for quantum technology. Progress continues in each technology type so monitoring media will be critical for business decision makers in future.

Chapter 4

A Brief History of Quantum Computing

"If you think you understand quantum mechanics, you don't understand quantum mechanics" - Richard Feynman, former American theoretical physicist & Caltech Professor

Despite the suggestion in the media that quantum computing is a new technological phenomenon, components of the field have been around for forty years (1981 to 2021) and in quantum mechanics for much longer. This chapter provides an overview of the timeline of events taking place during that period through the creative activities of numerous scientists, engineers, philosophers, and business people in the development of the quantum computer.

We will start somewhat further back than 1981. In the twentieth century as early as the 1900's through 1940's, quantum theorists reigned, people like Niels Bohr, Max Planck and Albert Einstein articulating the possibilities of quantum physics and mechanics. In Einstein's case, he referred to the quantum phenomenon as "spooky action at a distance". By 1973, researchers and scientists, like Alexander Holevo, were publishing papers illustrating that n qubits could carry a greater amount of information than the same number of classical bits. In

1975, R. P. Poplavskii released his paper titled "Thermodynamical models of information processing" illustrating the potential to simulate quantum systems on classical computers.

For many, the true start of today's quantum computation occurred for our purposes, at what many consider the birthplace of quantum computing, Caltech (Pasadena California) and the May 6, 1981 lecture by physicist Richard Feynman. During this lecture, Feynman outlined the possible advantages of leveraging quantum systems for computation to simulate nature. Feynman, a thought leader in quantum mechanics (the study of physics at the smallest small scale), was arguably the first scientist to understand the implication of electrons and photons sometimes behaving like particles and sometimes like waves. Such behaviour did not appear to obey the laws of nature humans generally accepted. Feynman understood, based on arguments published by Niels Bohr and Albert Einstein in the early part of the 20th century, that measuring something may or may not affect their state.

In fact, by Feynman's time, it was understood that electrons and photons could be, until they were measured, in both states at once, or in two places at the same time or what is referred to as superposition. Yet it was Feynman who realised the implication of being able to simulate the realities of the miniscule, not in bits of 1's and 0's but in a form to simulate the complexities of nature. A computer that would simulate quantum mechanics.

By 1985, the first description of a universal quantum computer was issued by Oxford University's David Deutsch, a computer able to simulate any other quantum computer with at most a polynomial slowdown, while error-correction schemes were being recommended by Asher Pers. The University of Oxford continued to play an important part in quantum development through Artur Ekert who proposed entanglement-based secure communication.

Two now very famous names in the quantum algorithm world are Grover and Shor. Peter Shor, a famous name in the world of quantum computing, is an MIT Professor of Applied Mathematics. His algorithm, Shor's algorithm, developed in 1994, factors exponentially faster than existing traditional computer algorithms. Lov Grover, an Indian-American scientist, in 1996, proposed an algorithm for unstructured search that "finds with high probability the unique input to a black box function that produces a particular output value." Shor and Grover's algorithms form the basis of many of today's approaches to quantum computing.

Fast forward to 2010, in which year I read a publication by Thaddeus Ladd and team in *Nature* entitled 'Quantum Computers'. The concept fascinated me 11 years ago. While the article obviously didn't answer all the questions for a technology that is only now coming to the fore, it set in motion for me a journey of technology discovery. Ten years later, Ladd would comment on new research in quantum computing that was game-changing. In this case, it was an Australian team who sought to control the atomic nuclei embedded in silicon (think microchip materials) through electric fields, to control the quantum bits, or qubits, in a super powerful quantum computer. The game changer? Controlling the primary element of a quantum computer the same way we do with transistors in a traditional microchip.

The Last Decade

At the start of the last decade in 2011, D-Wave claimed development of quantum annealing, the first commercially available quantum computer, introducing their product called D-Wave One. Repetitive error correction was demonstrated in a quantum processor, and diamond quantum computer memory was demonstrated.

In 2012, a working transistor was created from a single atom, researchers found a method for manipulating the charge of nitrogen vacancy-centres in diamond, and the first 300 qubit/particle quantum simulator was reported. 1QB Information Technologies (1QBit) was founded and billed as the "World's first dedicated quantum computing software company."

In 2013, a qubit was maintained in superimposed state for ten times longer than what has ever been achieved before, and a large-scale quantum algorithm using explicit fault-tolerant, error-correction protocols was developed for factoring.

In 2014, Japanese and Australian researchers published the first large-scale quantum computing architecture for a diamond-based system, scientists, via quantum teleportation, transferred data over a distance of 10 feet with zero percent error rate, a crucial step towards a quantum Internet and Nike Dattani & Nathan Bryans broke the record for the largest number factored on a quantum device: 56153 (breaking the previous record - 143).

2015 discoveries included quantum information encoded by simple electrical pulses. quantum error detection code using a square lattice of four superconducting qubits, D-Wave Systems Inc.'s announcement that it had broken the 1,000-qubit barrier, and the successful development of a two-qubit silicon logic gate.

In 2016, MIT scientists along with physicist Rainer Blatt leveraged an ion-trap computer to efficiently implement Shor's algorithm. In the same year, the IBM Quantum Experience was launched providing an online interface to superconductive computers.

In 2017, Microsoft launched its Q Sharp quantum programming language integrated with Visual Studio, and D-Wave Systems Inc. announced "general commercial availability of the D-Wave 2000Q quantum annealer," with 2000 qubits. In the same year, China announced a 2,000 kilometer quantum communication network using quantum cryptography between Beijing and Shanghai.

2018 saw Intel begin testing on a silicon-based spin-qubit processor, and the US signed into law the National Quantum Initiative Act, "establishing the goals and priorities for a 10-year plan to accelerate the development of quantum information science and technology applications in the United States".

In 2019, IBM launched its largest quantum computer at the time at 53 qubits and Google became the first to claim quantum supremacy.

In 2020, progress was made in quantum noise reduction by institutions in Australia and the US using machine learning "taking quantum noise in a quantum chip down to 0%." The development of artificial atoms (with higher number of electrons) in silicon quantum dots produced more stable qubits making silicon-based technology reusable in the quantum era. In communication, researchers established a method to "correct for signal loss in a prototype quantum node that can catch, store and entangle bits of quantum information" which could extend quantum networks distance. Silicon figured into other research that could permit less cooling, and thus reduced operating cost and may enable "integrating classical control electronics with the qubit array." Extending coherence (universal coherence protection) also factored into the year's progress via the Argonne National allowing quantum systems to remain "operational (or "coherent") for 10,000 times longer than before."

Today

Here in 2021, the momentum continues. New applications, new discoveries, new investments. There has been a flurry of activity in China with researchers reporting the quantum network started in 2017 was now the "world's largest integrated quantum communication network, combining over 700 optical fibers with two QKD-ground-to-satellite links for a total distance between nodes of the network of networks of up to ~4,600 km." In the first instance of entangling particles between two moving devices, Chinese researchers successfully entangled photons between drones. IonQ announced it would become the first pure public quantum computing company. Many more 2021 advances are discussed later in the book.

Bob Sorenson, an analyst at Hyperion Research, stated the world's quantum computing market in 2019 totalled about $250 million. Less than a single day of ad revenue for Alphabet (Google's parent company). IDC, a data research firm, predicted quantum computing will be adopted by 25% of Fortune Global 500 companies by 2023 and Gartner forecast 20% would be budgeting for QC projects versus 1% in 2020. Throughout this book, you will read about examples of quantum progress and how these investments are making an impact. Also, we will look at use cases for quantum computing that are not years away. These are current demands for a transformational technology being fast-tracked by an increasing number of researchers and vendors. Beyond these use cases for applied quantum computing, there are a myriad of other opportunities in longevity, self-driving vehicles, molecular research and more. The technology field is ripe for quantum developments, and businesses should be ready to take advantage of quantum capabilities now and into the future.

As a former business executive, I had always been intrigued by how organizations could move repetitive, manual tasks into the realm of the computer and engage people in more value-add, often less dangerous activities. Such pursuits fired my interest in artificial intelligence. Yet, over the last few years, I encountered numerous problems (business and otherwise) that could benefit from even faster processing, over and above the convergence of the human mimicry of artificial intelligence, cloud computing and more recently 5G line speed.

Complex analysis with hundreds of variables on traditional computers takes time. Time which translates into cost. Cost in dollars and cost sometimes in lives. Challenges for traditional computing capabilities surface as groups push the extremes of scale and complexity relating to a universe of human and organizational problems. Only time will tell how well quantum computing addresses such issues.

Chapter 5

The Global Quantum Landscape

While not mainstream for today's technology stacks, some argue the field is overhyped. Scott Aaronson, American theoretical computer scientist and David J. Bruton Jr. Centennial Professor of Computer Science at the University of Texas at Austin, recently argued on his blog that "Many of the companies making wildly overhyped claims are recognized leaders of the field".

Yet, quantum computing is making a global push for acceptance through applications and public and private investment and research. According to the World Government Forum, "Quantum computing is moving from the high-tech lab to mainstream commercial use over the next few years, representing the next major breakthrough in modern IT." The Yahoo Report on Global Quantum Computing Market by Technology, Infrastructure, Services and Industry Verticals (2020-2025) suggests that the market for QC hardware by 2025 will hit $6.2 billion primarily focusing on simulation, optimization, and sampling in industry verticals like finance, energy, and transportation.

Founding and patent activity in the past 10 years in quantum computing has benefitted from increased investment globally both by governments and by industry. Funding for most Europe and Asia start-ups in the past five years have been from public funding, while US companies funding originated mostly from private equity and venture capital. Large investment rounds continue in the current year (for example Xanadu's USD 100 million). Less than 10% of investment generally has been directed towards non-hardware targets.

Quantum Activities Today

So what is happening in the quantum world in 2021?

- Growing a standards-based quantum community
- Making quantum more available to diverse groups of users
- Investing billions from both public and private sources
- Providing learning opportunities online
- Combining classical and quantum technologies seamlessly
- Broadening the use case applications
- Increasing number and kind of developers
- Offering open source (like the Unitary Fund and Qiskit)
- Offering cloud-native deployment
- Improving security through quantum cryptography
- Developing quantum ethics – i.e. military uses, and human DNA
- Doubling and tripling of participants at conferences
- More quantum conferences like Quantum Business Europe, Quantum Computing Summit and Quantum.Tech

National Initiatives

At a country or government level, numerous countries have entered into quantum programmes including the U.S. National Quantum Initiative Act 2018, Canada, in its 2021 budget announced over CAD $360 million for the newly established National Quantum Strategy, there's Quantum Industry Canada and the World Economic Forum's Global Future Council on

Quantum Computing. Brazil hosts the Quantum Computing Group at the National Laboratory for Scientific Computing. Quantum Leap Africa incorporates institutions from South Africa, Senegal, Ghana, Cameroon, Tanzania, and Rwanda. Seven countries have committed over USD $1billion each for their respective quantum research and development, China's public investment is fully $10 billion in their National Laboratory for Quantum Information Sciences alone, the EU over $4 billion, the USD over $2 billion and Canada $1 billion. The Netherlands recently pledged over 600 million euros to their national quantum program. With real-world application, corporate investment and government sponsorship, quantum computing's progress should accelerate.

One measure of global quantum activity is in the number of patents being issued in each country. Between June 2020 and May 2021, the US – issuing the greatest number of patents globally – increased 17%, while China – currently in second but not for long – added 337% more patents in the same 1-year period (In China, a quantum powerhouse combination now exists - The Chinese Academy of Sciences partnered with Alibaba Group's cloud computing subsidiary, to create the Alibaba Quantum Computing Laboratory which combines Alibaba's cloud computing and algorithms skills and the academy's quantum artificial intelligence expertise).

Japan's improvement in patents was next at 206% followed by Germany at 123%. Canada is in fourth with total number of patents but its pace has slowed according to statistics provided by Michael Kurek, member of Le Lab Quantique. Clearly some governments are prioritizing quantum computing science & research and they're committing to the field with major investments.

Europe's Push Towards the Quantum Future

My focus over the past few years has been the intersection of artificial intelligence, IoT and quantum computing (QC) through experience and observation. Experiencing the evolution of quantum technology here in Canada through consulting with scaling companies considering quantum computing as part of their arsenal. Observing companies like D-Wave Systems and ecosystems like The Institute for Quantum Computing (IQC), a scientific research institute at the University of Waterloo.

Yet in 2021, one geographic region has continuously appeared on my quantum radar. Europe. Europe's strides in 2021 have been remarkable. Announcement after announcement about country-originated investments appear weekly. For a relatively new and what some would consider unproven technology, countries in Europe are embracing quantum computing at a furious pace. While we constantly hear about the world QC leadership of the US and China (and their national investments exceed all others), the trends include a notable European flavor.

Take France and Germany for example. The headline in ScienceBusiness.net this month read "France and Germany line up for quantum leap". What kind of leap? A €1.8B strategy and a €2B programme respectively towards research and commercialization. Germany plans to invest the €2 billion in building its first quantum computer and related applications with the largest portion - €720 million - going to the German Aerospace Centre (DLR - the national aeronautics and space research centre).

Quantum Delta NL Example

I'm a member of several quantum meetup communities around the world including Quantum Amsterdam. Recently the early-stage group helped promote a newly approved

DutchGrowth program. In August 2019, the Dutch National Agenda for Quantum Technology was created, followed by Quantum Delta NL (QDNL) which will drive the use of €615 million in funding to accelerate quantum technology development in the Netherlands.

The focus of QDNL will be quantum computation/simulation, development and deployment of quantum networks and applications in quantum sensing. QDNL will leverage funds to support start-ups and spin-offs, translate their efforts into educational topics, expanding the quantum ecosystem and drive dialogue arounds the social aspects of quantum's impact. Interestingly, the Netherlands has the potential to be the first country in the world with a country-wide quantum internet given its relatively small area and quantum progress.

Quantum computing progress and maturity depends on the collaboration of government, academia, institutions and industry. In that vein, QDNL incorporates numerous institutions including TU Delft, QuSoft, TNO, QuTech and more as well as industry partners like ING, ABN-AMRO, Bosch, Intel, Ericsson and others. QDNL's model will be one to watch.

As one of my LinkedIn colleagues, a PhD from Harvard University, so appropriately pointed out, "as scientists in the field, we need to be very careful to not overpromise on R&D speed and applications…". As an Artificial Intelligence strategist for large and small companies, I regularly cautioned business leaders about the hype, bias and project challenges associated with AI. The same factors apply to quantum computing, yet as my colleague concluded "…it is an exciting time as institutions commit resources to exploring these questions. And European pioneers are braving this new world regardless of the multitude of challenges ahead.

Not to be left out, Austria recently announced the "Austrian Quantum Fiber Network" or AQUnet. AQUnet is a fiber-optic network spanning the country to permit the secure exchange of quantum information and precision measurements with a 2.8million euro initial outlay from the Research Promotion Agency FFG.

Finnish-based IQM Computers uses a hardware-software co-design approach and bills itself as "the European leader in superconducting quantum computers" with deals announced with the German Ministry of Research and Education and its host country Finland. IQM is involved in the public-private collaboration underway (powered by € 20.7 million in funding from The Ministry of Economic Affairs and Employment) with VTT Technical Research Centre of Finland.

In Spain, the Spanish National Research Council (CSIC) coordinates over two dozen quantum research efforts within the country. Including affiliations with groups like the Quantum Information and Foundations Group (QUINFOG), and BBVA working on financial algorithms. As well, Spain hosts The Institute of Photonic Sciences (ICFO) in Catalonia.

Conferences focused on quantum computing in large and small sizes abound. Meetings called "Stammtisch's" (or regular table directly translated to English) and Meetup groups occur in multiple European cities including Munich, Madrid, Amsterdam (including my colleagues at Quantum London). Full scale virtual conferences like Quantum Business Europe were held for the first time in 2021.

What is truly exciting for me, as a former financial services executive, is the commercialization potential for quantum computing. Despite being birthed in academic and industrial labs starting over 40 years ago with Richard Feynman and colleagues's first expressions about quantum, the technology has progressed significantly over the last half-decade. Pioneering firms have addressed optimization challenges like traffic flow in

Japan, and Covid health research globally. Others are applying QC to risk mitigation in trading, investment portfolios, and data security. Firms like Swiss-based ID Quantique are applying quantum cryptography services today. The list of complex challenges and applications are endless.

The European path to quantum competitiveness is being travelled through consortiums, local gatherings, academic curiosity and national investments on an increasing scale. Certainly, nations like China and the US have taken an early leadership position, yet it will be very interesting to watch over the next few years how the European magic appears on our screens.

The European quantum community regard themselves as leaders in community excellence through effective organization of large industry stakeholder groups and subgroups into the European Quantum Industry Consortium (QuIC). QuIC , launched February 4, 2021 with the objective to bring together these European quantum industry players for collaboration and fostering their common interests, is headquartered in Germany. Of the more than 100 members, two-thirds are small-medium enterprises and start-ups, the remainder being research centres and large industry players.

Quantum in the Government & Military

Quantum computing applications are not limited to researchers and industry. Section 214 of the U.S. National Defense Authorization Act of Fiscal Year 2021 directed each military department to identify opportunities for applying quantum technologies and engage with small and medium size businesses providing private sector capabilities to government and military applications. The timeline focus for the section is 1 to 3 years so.

The Advanced Technology Academic Research Center or ATARC, based in Virginia, is one of the organizations identifying opportunities for the military and they are numerous. Logistics, supply chain optimization, energy uses, maintenance schedules, cryptography, robotics, materials and medical applications over and above warfare simulations to name a few.

The US Air Force Research Laboratory (AFRL), for example, partnered in 2021 with QC Ware to leverage its software/algorithms to provide improved surveillance of unmanned aircraft. Countries are not only investing heavily in quantum computing, but they are also partnering with commercial entities to accelerate the delivery of quantum solutions.

A March 2021 paper from the University of Prague (UP) looked at quantum technology as not introducing fundamentally new technologies, rather materially improving the measurement, precision, efficiency and computational strength to existing military technologies. This UP report aims to review and map the possible quantum technology military applications to serve as the entry point for international peace and international security assessment, ethics research or military and governmental policy, strategy and decision making. Quantum technologies for military applications, introducing new capabilities, increasing effectiveness and improving precision lead to 'quantum warfare', wherein new military strategies, doctrines, policies and ethics should be established.

Multiple countries are promoting and funding government quantum initiatives. The National Quantum Initiative in the United States is billed as "The Federal Source and Gateway to Quantum R&D Across the U.S. Government" and it's internet address is quantum.gov. Signed into law on December 21, 2018, the purpose of the act is to "ensure the continued leadership of the United States in quantum information science and its technology applications. It provides for a coordinated Federal program to accelerate quantum research and development for the economic and national security of the United States." The European Quantum Consortium or QUIC advocates "advocates, promotes, and fosters the common interests of the European Quantum Industry towards all Quantum Technology stakeholders". The Centre for Quantum Technologies in Singapore is a Research Centre of Excellence hosted by the National University of Singapore and "brings together physicists, computer scientists and engineers to do basic research on quantum physics and to build devices based on quantum phenomena."

Each country or groups of countries (like the European Union) will be introducing their own quantum projects, standards, and regulations throughout the next decade. What will be interesting to watch is whether we will see convergence in those areas, supremacy in progress, and/or benefits for humanity that inspire younger generations to invest their time and careers in this field.

Is Quantum Strictly For Large Organizations?

If you're part of a smaller, innovative organization somewhere around the globe, can your firm engage in the quantum community? Are there communities to support development of your applications? Much like the AI community, quantum hubs are being launched all over the world. Organizations such The UK Quantum Simulation and Computing Hub, The Creative Destruction Lab in Toronto, and the Quantum Technology Innovation Hub (QTIH) at the University of Birmingham, as well as Canada's Interdisciplinary Institute for Technological Innovation and the MiQro Innovation Collaborative Center help accelerate commercialization of technologies. The IBM Quantum Hub at the University of Sherbrooke provides access to IBM resources as well as “amplifying the local quantum technology network by attracting companies to join and to adopt new technologies”.

You may have heard of ‘Quantum Valley’, which is a mass of institutions devoted to quantum progress in the Waterloo, Canada area. Composed of research, business and investment partners including the Institute for Quantum Computing of the University of Waterloo, the Perimeter Institute (theoretical quantum physics), the Waterloo Institute for Nanotechnology, the Lazaridis Institute, (management of technology entrepreneurs), and finally the Quantum Valley Investment and Quantum Valley Ideas Lab. If you’re leading a firm interested in quantum, Quantum Valley may be your destination.

Dedicated to women entrepreneurs, SheQ, is a platform with the objective of connecting women to the young, intriguing field of quantum computing.” Traditionally STEM has been a male dominated field, and the efforts of SheQ permits women to learn about quantum computing in a comfortable, motivating environment.

D-Wave Systems in Canada provides “training courses and resources to help organizations get started with quantum and we work with academic institutions around the world to reach the next generation of students, entrepreneurs, and researchers.” according to Murray Thom, VP of Product Management. So, vendors are recognizing the importance of extending their knowledge and services to organizations of all sizes.

The University of Maryland initiated a Quantum Business Incubator to “to nurture quantum-focused startups” with an initial $25 million investment. In Canada, the Creative Destruction Lab’s (CDL) Quantum Stream brings together leading companies like Zapata Computing, IBM, Rigetti, Xanadu and D-Wave “to build ventures in the emerging domain of quantum computing, machine learning, optimization, sensing and other applications of quantum technologies.” What’s exciting for smaller companies is that CDL offers a 4-week technical and business quantum bootcamp led by industry and academic leaders in quantum technologies and machine learning, followed by five objective-setting sessions and mentoring.

You'll find that meetup communities are also a great way to create your own network. Meetups, mostly free to join, are a great way to meet others interested in speaking, presenting and merely being curious about the field of quantum computing. Over 17,000 people in 74 quantum meetup communities in 55 cities from 20 different countries are connecting today.

Today, finding access to quantum computing support is much less of a challenge in the past for smaller organizations. Those listed are a fraction of what's available globally to gain entrance to the quantum field. Take some of the ideas from this book, and reach out to quantum communities and hubs to accelerate your own firms progress towards success.

Chapter 6

Quantum Supremacy, Advantage, Maturity & Convergence

"While quantum supremacy is an important milestone, it doesn't really have any practical value by itself. The real goal will be using quantum computing to enhance or even supercharge other efforts." John Breeden II. 2020

If you've been exposed to today's quantum technology media, you may have heard the term 'quantum supremacy'. Quantum supremacy occurs when a quantum system can solve a problem that no traditional computer is able to solve within a reasonable amount of time. This was the definition originated by John Preskill, professor of theoretical physics, in 2012. According to MIT, "the objective of quantum supremacy is to find computational problems that are feasible on a small-scale quantum computer but are hard to simulate classically. "

Google claimed quantum supremacy in 2019. IBM countered shortly thereafter. The problem selected by Google, some said, was one that played to the strengths of quantum computers and stumped traditional versions.

Google's original quantum supremacy claim stated they had developed a quantum computer capable of a computation that would take a traditional computer 10,000 years, yet completed in 200 seconds. One problem solved in 200 seconds, that would take a classical computer 10,000 years (or 2.5 days according to IBM). Still the improvement was material. And the race for not just supremacy but advantage was on.

This statement created a flurry of activity surrounding quantum supremacy, quantum advantage, and metrics on quantum performance. In late 2020, Chinese scientists claimed a breakthrough in quantum computing which suggested a photonic quantum computer (one based on light) had performed specific computations 100 trillion times faster than the most powerful supercomputer. That's trillion with a "T". Using Gaussian boson sampling, the prototype detected up to 76 photons where earlier attempts were limited to 5. Critics argued the technology did not have programmability, yet the numbers are staggering.

What's the difference between quantum supremacy and quantum advantage? We've defined supremacy through the lens of famed quantum expert John Preskill. Quantum advantage refers to "the moment when a quantum computer can compute hundreds or thousands of times faster than a classical computer" according to Manufacturing Business Technology magazine.

The essential equation in quantum computing is more qubits equals greater potential for building commercially viable applications. Over the past 20 years, the number of qubits in a functioning quantum computer has grown significantly. In 1999, IBM's collaboration with Oxford, MIT and Berkeley produced a 2-qubit computer. By the year 2006, a 12-qubit computer (this from the Institute of Quantum Computing, MIT, and the Perimeter Institute for Theoretical Physics) was in place. Two years later, D-Wave increased that count to 28, followed by the IBM et al group nine years later to 50 qubits in 2017. In 2019,

Dave Rigetti (a former IBM'er) and his team at Rigetti Computing bumped the number to 128 qubits.

Overtime, quantum computer manufacturers, much like their classical predecessors have added to the speed and fidelity through research, testing, discovery and more testing to add more qubits, less noise and greater fault tolerance.

The measurement for quantum computing performance has also evolved from straightforward number of qubits to IBM's quantum volume to IonQ's Algorithmic qubits to more recently DARPA's "yardsticks". IBM's approach attempted to provide a comparator to traditional computer transistor counts. The challenge in quantum environments is that qubits decohere in under a millisecond. The IBM Quantum Volume protocol tests "how well a quantum computer can run a circuit consisting of random two-qubit gates acting in parallel on a subset of the device's qubits." IBM, starting in 2019, had a qubit capacity of 27 qubits . By 2020 that number was 66. By 2021, the qubit capacity is expected to be 127, with 2022 and 2023 at 613 and 1121 respectively. IonQ takes it one step further in calculating the largest number of effectively perfect qubits one could deploy for a typical quantum program considering error correction as well.

Annealing computers count their qubits differently. D-Wave announced a system in 2020 where "...D-Wave is guaranteeing the availability of 5,000 qubits to Leap users using Advantage," with some variance chip to chip but a minimum of 5,000. Combine that with something called 15-way qubit connectivity, where each qubit is connected to 15 other qubits (typically that number is six) enabling the embedding of larger and more complex problems with fewer physical qubits.

DARPA's approach called 'The Quantum Benchmarking Broad Agency Announcement' seeks out "meaningful metrics to quantify how useful or transformative large quantum computers will actually be once they exist" according to The Quantum Daily.

As a business leader, quantum performance is just one metric you would consider in making your QC decision. I tend to take the practical approach and agree with John Breeden. The most important factor is can quantum computers supercharge your efforts?

Quantum Leaders Vying For Competitive Advantage

Do the names Jay Gould, Edward Harriman, Cornelius Vanderbilt or Collis P. Huntington mean anything to you? If you know a little about U.S. history, you'd know they were some of the most successful railroad tycoons of the 19th century.

So, what does that have to do with quantum leaders of today? Bear with me. Railroad tycoons of the 1850's-1890's like those named above pioneered in both technology and in geography (in this case the distance across America). The goal of delivering people and cargo across the nation on a Transcontinental Railroad was epic in its scope, budget and challenges. Yet these pioneering individuals took on the challenges and created a network of railways that criss-crossed the United States then and still do today.

"Many of the companies that dominate the internet today did not exist prior to its invention," says Paul Lipman, Chief Commercial Officer of Cold Quanta. "As quantum moves out of the R&D phase to true commercialization it will have an impact every bit as profound, defining the next generation of leaders across multiple industries." So true. And a new generation of quantum leaders.

Michael Kurek, member of Paris-based Think Tank Le Lab Quantique, published an infographic of the companies currently involved in quantum computing. The infographic held over 500 companies. The quantum ecosystem is growing and quantum offerings abound.

Today's leaders of quantum computing companies (people like Chad Rigetti of Rigetti Computing, Alan Baratz of D-Wave Systems Inc., Tony Uttley at Honeywell, Peter Chapman/Christopher Monroe/Jungsang Kim at IonQ, Chris Savoie (and founding team) at Zapata Computing, and Robin Li/Eric Xu at Baidu are paving the way to the world's newest railroad, the quantum internet/quantum communication, with their increasingly fast and increasingly accurate quantum computers and links to nodes and networks.

It took decades for the railroad tycoons of the 19th century to lay down enough track to cover the whole of the United States. And while arguably the concept of quantum computing has been around for decades, the traction in the last year (despite the pandemic restrictions) has been nothing short of miraculous and forecasts for real quantum computing applications are shortening every day. Alan Baratz would argue it's here today as the leader of one of, if not the earliest, commercial quantum system.

Now while the railroad tycoons of the second half of the 19th century had rather poor reputations as 'robber barons', they were still pioneers in pushing railroad technology and track mileage. The New York Central, the Union Pacific, the Chesapeake & Ohio, the Wabash and Great Northern were all components of the US experiment and implementation of rail travel. In 1840, the United States had just 2,800 miles of track according to americanrails.com. By 1916 that number had increased almost 100-fold to 254,000 miles.

Consider the key metrics in the quantum world of numbers of qubits, quantum volume (the measure that incorporates accuracy as well), economy in terms of cost, size of the computer (from room size to, in time some argue, the size of an Xbox). In terms of qubits, ion trap quantum computers are claiming hundreds of quits, while quantum annealing computers (today considered ideal for problems like optimization) can be as high as 5,000 qubits (recall D-Wave Advantage). And that's the numbers today. Imagine what quantum computing power will be like in 5 years.

This year's Quantum for Business conference (called Q2B20) brought together many of these increasingly familiar names in the world of Quantum Computing. Maybe not surprisingly, they each had a slightly different story to tell about their offerings, yet when one considers the sum total of their message it is remarkable. A global community of PhD's, visionaries, and enthusiastic, hard workers in all functions (akin to the engineers, steel manufacturers and labourers of the railway industry) are driving towards unforeseen potential of solving problems like climate change, traffic flow, cybersecurity and especially important today, molecular research for healthcare solutions.

According to Boston Consulting Group, companies assume four roles across layers of the stack in the quantum computing ecosystem. They divide up the industry between end-to-end providers, hardware and system players, software & services players, and specialists who operate at various stack levels. Those levels include quantum computing hardware, systems, system software, applications and services and industry players move between these layers depending upon opportunity.

Better known hardware manufacturers like D-Wave Systems Inc. (the Canadian company who started up in 1999), uses quantum annealing as their primary approach to computing. IBM, IonQ, Rigetti, and Honeywell are other well-established hardware manufacturers. Established software and service specialists include Zapata Computing, Cambridge Quantum Computing, QC Ware, 1Qbit, and Riverlane.

There are plenty of companies seeking the leadership in quantum performance (whereas just 5 years ago that number was a fraction of today). Specialist companies include Tellus Matrix Group, Quantika, Entanglement partners, Quantum Benchmark, Q-CTRLSeeQC, Silicon Quantum Computing, PsiQ, and Alpine Quantum Technologies. Many of these companies are university spin-offs, subsidiaries of larger entities and partnerships of academic and corporate entities.

And each would offer you a vision of today's capabilities and tomorrow's goals via a roadmap. Roadmaps are in vogue. The desire from consumers (buyers of such hardware) to gain some comfort in when a viable, reliable product will become available. Today's Noisy Intermediate Scale Quantum (NISQ) computers claim adequacy for very specific problems. Fully error-corrected quantum computing is at least 5 years away if you listen to Google, PsiQ and Ion Q. The major hardware vendors are all targeting large scale error-corrected, fault tolerant quantum processing units by the year 2030 in their respective roadmaps.

For companies who are currently sitting on the sidelines, simply watching the activity in quantum computing from afar, it may soon be too late. Your competitors are getting involved, and by the time your team gets engaged, the train may have already left the station.

Quantum Maturity

The question I'm often asked is "how mature is quantum technology"? Relative to other technologies like integrated-circuit based CPU/GPU classical computer technology – quantum is not very mature. Between use cases of quantum there are vast differences in maturity (ie optimization vs others). Amount of investment is another measure. Number of users still another. Between industries, still greater variance exists in maturity (ie Finance vs Construction).

BCG in its Quantum Computing Report labelled various industries on a matrix of business value versus expected timing of quantum advantage. The industries with the lowest business value and longest expected timing to advantage (referred to as 'observers') were energy, and two cross-industry capabilities –

logistics and cybersecurity. Observers are monitoring what's happening in the quantum computing ecosystem and looking for business potential. Those with high business value yet longer expected timing (called 'followers') were in pharma and finance. Followers participate in quantum computing networks and seek to gain experience. Those low in business value yet shorter timing (or 'riders') included industrial goods and energy and areas of highly inefficient processes. Riders actively engage with the quantum ecosystem and lead their own efforts according to BCG. Finally there are the 'racing teams' who should have high business value and shorter expected timing to quantum advantage – those being chemistry and high-tech cross industry skills deploying machine learning and AI. Racing teams build out superior networks and lead by launching new offerings.

Yet another way to look at quantum maturity is by individual players. Here we present two views of quantum maturity. One from McKinsey & Co (the global consulting firm) and another from Sia Partners, a quantum lab providing quantum solutions as an intermediary between quantum technology firms and corporate users.

McKinsey proposes a five-level maturity scale with the first level being bystanders. *Bystanders* are the group of industry participants not exploring any activities in quantum computing. In terms of their adoption of technology, industries like healthcare systems and services (excluding healthcare researchers and pharma), professional services and governmental/public and social services.

The next level of maturity is called *Beginners*. Beginners may have established partnerships or consortia to explore QC use cases but not implemented any initiatives yet. Industries in the beginner category include consumer, insurance, travel, transport, logistics, energy and materials. Again not to suggest there are no use cases for quantum in these industries or pioneers or early adopters. Rather these beginners have, as a group, yet to engage in the new technology.

Learners form the next group. At this stage of maturity, the companies engage in competitive efforts and hiring quantum scientists or other roles devoted to quantum capabilities. At present, industries include automotive manufacturing and assembly, chemicals, pharmaceuticals, medical products, aerospace and defense and financial services. Some organizations, like the US Air Force are heavily engaged in quantum activities, however the comment here is that most entities in these industries qualify as learners.

Professionals, the fourth of five stages of quantum computing maturity, according to McKinsey, are starting to understand the impact of the technology through proprietary applications and developing a QC strategy. Much like in the evolution of AI, telecommunications, media and pure technology companies form this category.

Finally, *Legends*, the highest level of current quantum computing maturity, lead the innovation in QC applications. These companies are not associated with a specific industry. Overall McKinsey, found through its 2021 study, that the adoption rate of quantum computing was 2.9 out of 5. It will be interesting to monitor the change in that adoption rate over the next decade as the commercialization of the technology evolves.

Sia Partners (SP) considers quantum maturity a four-stage paradigm with the first stage being "*Not Explored*". This stage is self-explanatory, with members who have merely read about the technology in the media, and representing according to Sia Partners about 80% of the population of corporates from all industries.

Stage 2, '*Exploring*', refers to corporates investigating the impact of quantum computing both from those who have implemented it and for alignment with their own corporate goals. 10% of corporates are in this category. '*Experimenting*', the third stage, includes small teams or programs conducting proof of concepts applying early stage technology and represents approximately another 10%. Finally, '*Maturing*' is the final stage in the SP model, where corporates engage in larger scale programs in hybrid technology environments in production and begin organizational transformation. This group represents less than 1% of all corporates.

By these definitions of maturity, a time/maturity bell curve representing the various industries and entities would be highly left-ward skewed today. Yet through the efforts of a broad group of organizations (academic, government and industry) globally, those maturity levels may progress quickly over the next decade.

As a business leader or professional, it would be valuable to consider where your business rests today within these maturity scales, where your priorities align with quantum computing, and finally how and when the quantum computing industry will mature.

Contributors to Quantum Maturity

In order for quantum computing to mature as an industry and a technology there are a variety of factors which must be at play in parallel.

1. Standards – institutions with responsibility for developing technology standards like the US National Institute of Standards and Technology or NIST and its peers in other nations should be collaborating on key standards for quantum technology to not only progress the field but also to provide standards for reliable quantum technology going forward worldwide. National Quantum groups like Quantum.gov (US - official website of the U.S. National Quantum Coordination Office or NQCO), QED-C (US - Quantum Economic Development Consortium), QUIC (EU), QWorld (a global network of individuals, groups,

and communities) and Quantum Industry Canada (QIC) are investigating collaboration opportunities across national and international borders.

2. Multiple technologies in search of optimal QC – superconducting, photonics, topological, annealing, trapped ion, neutral atoms, and any new types – push to find the best technology option(s) for each use case.

3. Talent – the quantum technology field is in pursuit not just of PhD's but as Ruslan Yunusov of the Russian Quantum Center says the field needs people with business acumen who can bridge the two skills; Teams building quantum solutions also require diversity by age, gender, race, background, experience, and personality to succeed.

4. Education – programs increasingly are in-place or being developed for future quantum employees and quantum careers such as CERN, IBM, and other institutions.

5. Accessibility – quantum computing is like any other field in that it must have ease of use and accessibility by users. Developing interfaces that make quantum accessible is a priority. One can look to IBM's Qiskit availability and IonQ's work in leveraging Qiskit across quantum types.

6. Investment – early numbers suggest investment may not be a barrier unless significant results and ROI are not achieved in the near term. Venture capital firms seeking an exit depend on companies to achieve forecast goals and not simply push back milestones. Governments expect to see job creation, economic and social benefits from their investment. According to The Quantum News,

"over the past five years not only has there been a boom in the number of quantum computing start-ups but a significant shift in the funding landscape, away from hardware focused entities towards those focused on software/algorithm development." The evolving focus from hardware to software aligns closely with the classical computing evolution in the 1970's onward.

7. New Milestones & Early Wins – Today's grand challenge is to reach 1 million qubits. Early win examples include Samsung quantum random number generator security enabled smartphones with ID Quantique QRNG chips. The world needs to push new milestones, research wins and production wins to keep the momentum going forward for quantum technology.

Notwithstanding the many potential barriers to achieving a universal error-corrected, fault tolerant quantum computer at a reasonable cost to its consumers with global accessibility, there are so many quantum enthusiasts in the world today versus five years ago. I'm excited for the field of quantum technology and optimistic it will continue to mature. One question to resolve is will these quantum technologies converge and will one be pronounced the winner?

Convergence vs Dominance

History is riddled with examples of technological convergence into one appliance, one standard, one protocol or one alignment of technologies. One of the most famous is the smartphone where previously distinct elements such as the camera, email or SMS communication, the telephone, Internet and data access, watching video, game playing, music and a myriad of computer applications converged into one physical appliance sharing common digital electronics and software.

The digital world experienced convergence in at least three distinct ways according to Jakki Mohr in the 2010 publication "Marketing of High-technology Products and Innovations". Mohr comments that "previously stand-alone devices are being connected by networks and software, significantly enhancing functionalities; previously stand-alone products are being converged onto the same platform, creating hybrid products in the process; and companies are crossing traditional boundaries such as hardware and software to provide new products and new sources of competition."

Another comes in the form of computer networks in which a multiplicity of operating systems is able to communicate via different protocols. Viewing the same media from many different devices (like a desktop, laptop, mobile phone, tablet) is another form of convergence. Converging digital simulations with games, video and information creates augmented and virtual reality. Educational instruction converged with the internet, computers and web meeting capability to create online learning which leaped forward as an acceptable mode in the last year due to the pandemic. Smart TV's compete with laptop streaming in offering a traditional TV viewing experience yet with the choice and features of streaming. Healthy in-home activity has been transformed by convergence of mirror-like devices with machine learning and camera technology. Douglas Mulhall, science journalist, in his book "Our Molecular Future: How Nanotechnology, Robotics, Genetics and Artificial Intelligence Will Transform Our World" describes the pending convergence of these technologies expected to transform our world. The question is will quantum follow the digital path?

Dominance is a very different concept. Take for example the battle between VHS and Beta technologies in the 1990's. Both provided viewers with the ability to watch video on tape to played in a video recorder or VCR. Sony bet heavily on the Beta version of VCR tapes yet over time VHS version won out, and the majority of VCR's played that technology. Digital photos now dominate over film. Streaming of movies and series are becoming more widely available on specialty channels online versus the traditional cable channels. Dominance of one technology over another or many others has also occurred throughout history. What will quantum computing's path be between convergence and dominance?

Quantum Convergence vs Dominance

Quantum computing is another example of convergence itself – convergence of quantum physics, math, traditional and new technologies. In quantum information science today there exists the convergence of science with technology in a multitude of ways. Quantum physics brings the concept of a qubit, entanglement and superposition. Mathematics brings quantum algorithms for factoring. Computer science brings the concepts of error correction, noise reduction and hybrid solving opportunities.

What factors will go into quantum convergence?

- Quantum algorithms requiring certain standards or built-in flexibility to operate on any quantum type.
- Supercooled vs room temperature machines?
- Availability of qubits
- Qubit volume
- Gate fidelity and qubit coherence
- Error correction capabilities
- Quantum regulations – which will meet the standards? Who issues the regulations? EU groups like QUIC, US groups like NIST and DARPA? Other countries? What about international standards?

- Quantum Benchmarks – DARPA is leading the effort to determine relevant benchmarks for quantum performance – who will achieve and maintain those benchmarks?
- How broadly quantum services are available by technology (think QIoT, QSaaS, QIaaS, and QPaaS, Quantum Cloud and Quantum Artificial Intelligence)
- Will there be a preponderance of adaptors required?
- Will RSA security be superseded by Quantum Cryptography, when and what are the implications?
- Will field-based solutions for hybrid-solvers be available and optimize the solutions in real time?

As we noted earlier, we're seeing different quantum technologies converge. IBM's Qiskit (originating in the quantum superconducting world) with IonQ's quantum computer (based on ion-trap technology) is one example. There are numerous varieties of quantum computers out there (add annealing, photonics, nitrogen vacancy diamonds, quantum dots and neutral atoms to #iontrap and #superconducting), which can be confusing for business #decisionmakers hoping to take advantage of the relatively new tech. When we see an example of convergence, it's an exciting proposition. IonQ, the first pure quantum company planning to go to public, announced on April 12th that "it is integrating its quantum computing platform with the open-source Qiskit software development kit" which was originally based on superconducting quantum computers.

Looking forward, by 2026 the global quantum computing market is forecast to growing at a compound annual growth rate exceeding 30% according to Report Linker.com If you're interested in technology of the future, quantum computing is the place to be. But which quantum technology?

Quantum's Trillion Dollar Question - Dominance

I often get asked the question by business people which quantum system will ultimately become the industry standard? At this point in time it's much too early to say. With advances being made daily in each of the quantum technologies profiled in this book, each have a chance at that standard. The opportunity means trillions of dollars in revenue potential in the future for the winner or winners.

Some believe that the first-out-of-the gate superconducting systems will prevail, while other argue that technologies requiring only room temperature processing, like ion-trap, will succeed. Carl Williams of NIST has been quoted saying. "I think the ions are better for the quantum repeaters because they don't need to have a refrigerator every 50 kilometers. But, if the cryo-manufacturers can build a 5-watt device that's small enough for a quantum repeater, superconducting could win that race, too. It's hard to say when those breakthroughs are going to come."

Mr. Williams is certainly correct breakthroughs will continue coming and the quantum industry will continue to publish at a furious pace. That being the case, organizations need to start planning for incorporating quantum technology sooner than later. Organizations who are not successfully implementing artificial intelligence are challenged to keep the pace of those who do. The same will apply to those not elevating quantum computing to their priority in the next few years. Quantum-Computing-as-a Service is not unrealistic in that time period and the organizations whose infrastructures are ready for it will excel. Hopefully we have demonstrated that progression that quantum computing is the next thing in technology and that the time to plan is now.

Chapter 7

What Problems Are Quantum Computing Suited For?

As a business leader or professional any technology investment must have value in solving your biggest problems whether internal or customer-facing. Quantum is a relatively new technology with great promise and one that could provide competitive advantages. So, there are several ways to consider a response to the question of what problems quantum computing are best suited for. We can consider the functions QC is suited to, or industry applications types, so we will look at both.

Today's quantum computers are suited for many application problems including optimization, cryptography, simulation, sampling and machine learning. Optimization occurs when given a set of constraints and optimization criteria a system finds the optimal variable combination from a virtually infinite number of combinations. We'll cover optimization in the chapter on Finance. Machine learning becomes optimized when the data becomes increasingly reliable, distributed and real time via quantum computing.

Sampling refers to an agent drawing values from a solution space allowing generalizations regarding the population distribution. Scientists from the University of Science and Technology of China, Hefei, have collaborated to achieve a significant milestone in sampling by creating an optical system with quantum computational power sampling in minutes where a classical computation would take hours to verify results. The boson sampling experiment sends 20 indistinguishable photons through an interferometer, measuring how 14 emerge from the other side. Solving this problem translates into predicting a vast distribution set. "After unavoidable losses in the system, the researchers found that they could routinely detect up to 14 photons per run, yielding an output with 3.7×1014 degrees of freedom. This enormous possibility space—ten orders of magnitude greater than that achieved previously…"

Cryptography refers to encrypting information at the physical network layer. We'll cover cryptography in the chapter on Security. Simulation refers to forward looking forecasts to assess various scenarios for decision-making, and we explore that later in this chapter.

Use Cases by Industry

- Finance – portfolio optimization, encryption, option pricing and Monte Carlo simulation.
- Logistics – real time disruption modelling, supply chain optimization, dynamic route optimization
- Chemicals – molecular dynamics simulation, protein folding prediction, quantum finite element method, chemical docking for product design, catalysis multiscale modelling
- Pharma - molecular dynamics simulation, protein folding prediction, prediction of pharmacokinetics, solubility,

toxicity and dosing, personalized medicine, generation of missing data, continuous progression monitoring in real time
- Aerospace and Defence – structural mechanics finite element method, cybersecurity, navigation
- Navigation – sensors in space, time clocks, hyper precise GPS

Quantum Simulation

Years ago, I enjoyed the sensation of flying aircraft on the Microsoft Flight Simulator. My first exposure was Flight Simulator 2.0 after its release in 1984. Some may remember at the time it being an incredible advance yet compared with Flight Simulator 2020, it was frankly rudimentary. Still, that is software evolution for you.

Regardless of the quality of the software, what Flight Simulator offered was a chance to experience something that occurs in the real world from your desktop or laptop. Each simulation incorporated factors like wind speed, wind direction, air speed, plane configuration, amount of flaps, remaining fuel, visibility and the list goes on.

No different are simulations to solve the world's biggest problems today like chemical combinations for fertilizer, development of recyclable materials, protein modelling for new vaccine solutions, innovations in human tissue replacement, superconductivity at room temperature and room pressure and more. Yet the challenge for scientists and researchers arises in the multitude of possible combinations resident in the Periodic Table of Elements (PTE). The PTE of metals, minerals and gases is arranged by atomic number, electron configuration, and recurring chemical properties, with 94 occurring naturally and 24 synthesized in labs.

Attempting to list all the combinations is one thing. Attempting to analyse the reactions of interactions of these combinations is quite another. The complexity of combinations and computations is almost infinite. Far beyond the capabilities of classical computing. Which is where quantum simulation enters the fray.

What's a simulation? A simulation is imitating a real-world system or process over a period of time. Starting with a model, which represents the dominant behaviours or characteristics the selected system or process, the simulation illustrates the evolution of the model over time.

Quantum simulation is one of the most promising routes to discovering new materials with new properties. For example, in the field of condensed matter physics which looks at the properties of solids and liquids and their atomic configuration, quantum simulation holds great promise. Certainly, the search for novel materials continues (no one can categorically state we have found them all), and the search incorporates many properties like:

- Strength
- Resistance to heat or cold
- Thickness
- Magnetism
- Electronics
- Interaction with light
- Permeability

And many more.

Take superconductivity for example. Superconductivity is important in things like magnetic resonance imaging (MRI) magnets and particle accelerators. Aluminum's properties allow for electricity to flow through the material with zero resistance when cooled to 1.75 Kelvin. The challenge is cooling it to 1.75K outside of the lab. So, quantum simulation could be used to search for combinations of elements that permit superconductivity at room temperature, and to do the search much faster than a traditional computer.

Simulations also must consider the chemistry aspect of combining elements together (such as the risk of a dangerous reaction in testing), so again quantum simulators could address the simulation of these interactions. Any errors, even infinitesimally small errors in the computation by classical computers, could lead to errors in the rate of chemical reaction and precision of interactions between electrons and atoms.

Progress Towards Quantum Simulation

In 2019, IonQ simulated water (H_20) molecules "with accuracy approaching what is needed for practical applications in the promising field of computational chemistry". In previous years, Google simulated hydrogen (2016) and IBM simulated lithium hydride and beryllium hydride (2017). D-Wave Systems Inc. recently announced their "Fully-programmable annealing quantum computer demonstrates 2 million times speed-up over classical CPU in a practical application" for a simulation of exotic magnetism. So, as one can see, there are existing precedents for simulating molecules/atoms today that offer hope for additional discoveries.

NVIDIA recently announced quantum simulation on GPUs through their SDK (Software Development Kit) called cuQuantum. The benefit? Error-free simulation on a classical computer technology by users hoping to investigate the basic logic without being challenged by noisy qubits increasing uncertainty when analyzing the results of a run. Such an approach could reduce research time in preparing for a full quantum simulation.

Classical computers have been largely capable of achieving the same speeds as early-stage quantum computers. As the number and fidelity of qubits increase, quantum computers begin to surpass onventional and super-computer technology. Researchers believe that until there is a 60-qubit quantum computer, leveraging hybrid quantum machine learning and classical computers could compete in processing. Still, eventually classical computers will be overtaken – a 100-qubit quantum computer would require a classical hard drive composed of all the atoms in the universe.

In terms of quantum computing hardware progress, IBM's recent roadmap announcement suggested they would be processing at over 1000 qubits by 2023. Both IBM and Google forecast over 1 million error-corrected qubits processing capability by 2030. These are phenomenal numbers compared to today's quantum computer capabilities (in the tens and hundreds), and are only some of the types of quantum technology available today.

Barriers to Quantum Simulation

According to David Isaac, founder of the Quantum News "Simulations will be one of the most important benefits of quantum computing. In the finance realm, quantum Monte Carlo simulations will have a profound impact." Still, in today's quantum computing reality, there are several barriers to the effective and efficient computational simulation of elements including:

- Implementing quantum error correction at scale
- Achieving these error-corrected qubit levels of quantum processing
- Discovering how to route wiring for 1 million qubits

- Leveraging simulations across all hardware platforms (superconducting, annealing, ion trap, photonics and any new approaches)
- Talent to run simulations
- Room temperature processing (seeing progress with photonic computers here)
- And many more

Yet when have barriers stopped humanity from the voyage of discovery? Quantum simulation appears inevitable and researchers and pioneers are pushing the edges of innovation to develop new materials and more importantly new solutions to support our own voyages of discovery. The exciting journey of those in the quantum computing field has really just begun. Better, faster, more accurate processors along with more experienced simulation talent and challenging problems to solve are a combination not unlike our forebears with better ships, more experienced crew and undiscovered seas to reach.

Chapter 8

The Quantum/Artificial Intelligence Duo

"As it pertains to AI/ML, I think what I'm most encouraged by is the potential for classical and quantum to work together leveraging the elastic nature of the cloud and the powerful, specific problem-solving capabilities of quantum computing."
Daniel Newman – Futurum Research

One of the things that quantum computing and artificial intelligence have in common is the ability to digest large amounts of data. According to IDC, a research marketing firm, the accelerating digitalization of our world is adding vast data stores (to the tune of 59 zettabytes – or 2 to the 70th power bytes). That number is forecast to experience a compound growth rate of 26% through 2024, where an individual business can generate terabytes of data by themselves every day.

How can we expect classical computers which are reaching the end of Moore's Law in integrated circuit growth, without fundamentally new technology? Many argue that technology comes from the infinitely small realm of quantum.

One of the aspects I recognized during the period from 2015 to 2020 about artificial intelligence was the evolution of thinking. In 2015, people were asking what is artificial intelligence? By 2020, they were asking how can I make artificial intelligence work for me? People in my network were devoting time to developing AI strategies, investigating new opportunities to be more competitive and finding talent to help drive those opportunities.

During that period, I wrote, also, about the overall quantum computing environment and the speed at which it was progressing globally. The same evolution is occurring with quantum computing as occurred with artificial intelligence. Now we are combining these two technologies intersecting at quantum machine learning.

Like classical computers, quantum versions also leverage algorithms to process that data. Quantum computing is the hardware layer. AI, the software thinking layer. Yet a relatively new phenomenon continues to evolve, namely quantum machine learning – the interaction of quantum algorithms and machine learning programs. In this hybrid situation, computationally difficult or expensive programs are outsourced to a quantum device. Classical data is encoded for quantum processing.

Can quantum computers run faster than traditional computers when using AI? That question today is too broad. Quantum computers are effective tools because they can process certain challenges that are impossible for traditional computers (even supercomputers) even with artificial intelligence. Yet AI and machine learning algorithms have been proven to be faster in certain instances using quantum computers. The magic for business is to understand how they can manage the hybrid traditional/quantum processing. AI and ML algorithms run on quantum computers means exponentially faster processing of data, which experientially makes models increasingly accurate in less time.

Want to enhance the quality of images generated with facial recognition? Leverage the processing power of quantum computing units or QPU's. According to the CEO of Zapata Computing, Chris Savoie, "quantum-enhanced generative models to enlarge this dataset with more images (both in terms of quantity and variety), which can significantly improve the detection model." The approach need not be restricted to image/face generation, the combination can be applied to molecules, cells, and medical scans.

Quantum machine learning models can consume data like images to achieve greater application to real world challenges. According to BBVA (Spanish multinational financial services company) researcher Samuel Fernández Lorenzo ,"Quantum machine learning can be more efficient than classic machine learning, at least for certain models that are intrinsically hard to learn using conventional computers." Fernández Lorenzo goes on to say "The most demanding task … in terms of computing workload and time consumption, is training the algorithm" and leveraging quantum processing "may contribute to developing an extremely powerful artificial intelligence in the future."

Want to run predictive analytics for financial modelling? Same recommendation. Refer to the chapter on Finance for more detail of portfolio optimization. Suffice to say, though, that when there are unpredictable outcomes based on a myriad of complex, dynamic factors, quantum computers have superior predictive capability.

Want to run natural language processing applications on a quantum computer? Ask world-renown quantum thought leader, CEO of Cambridge Quantum Computing (CQC) and 2020 Quantum Personality of the Year winner, Ilya Khan. When computers understand whole sentences in context, versus individual words, the computer is called meaning aware. Yet it is computationally very expensive to achieve real time speech without some guesswork. Quantum computing offers an opportunity for such efficiency. In fact, in March 2021, CQC announced the "Largest Ever Natural Language Processing Implementation on a Quantum Computer" running the first medium scale implementation of common NLP tasks. The effort paves the way "for the NLP community to engage with a quantum encoding of language processing." In April 2020, Khan made a bold prediction. "We could be as little as three years away from achieving a quantum advantage in AI if the largest players in the quantum computing space meet their goals."

The military in numerous countries have been exploring the intersection of artificial intelligence and quantum computing for the better part of the last decade. Machine learning is already in widespread use and research on battlefield robots is being conducted in over 50 countries according to J.R. Wilson writing for militaryaerospace.com in August 2020.

The most complex problems are now at our doorstep to be solved. Covid-19 is being fought with systems like Canada's D-Wave. Financial institutions like JP Morgan Chase leverage quantum computing to protect client accounts and make better investment choices. Where else is the technology being applied? Cybersecurity, drug development, battery advancement, cleaner fertilization, traffic optimization, weather forecasting and climate change.

By picking up this book, you have made your own 'quantum leap' into the future. Understanding the foundations of quantum computing, the players and the ecosystem should place you and your organization on firmer footing as you make decisions about this relatively new technology.

Chapter 9

Quantum Nodes, Networks & Internet

"Speed is the new currency of business" – Marc R. Benioff, Chairman and CEO, Salesforce

Prior to the advent of the internet of today, how did we communicate? Through phone (landline), physical mail, in-person. With the advent of the global internet in the early 1990's, email became a dominant communication method along with online posts and blogs. As the number of users grew, so did the amount of data being piped through the world wide web.

With foundations in the US Department of Defense Advanced Research Projects Agency (ARPA)'s ARPANET which was based on distributed networks of message blocks and packet switching, evolving into Transmission Control Protocol (TCP) and Internet Protocol (IP), the internet of today found it's feet in the world wide web conceived of by British computer scientist Tim Berners-Lee at CERN in Switzerland. The linking of hypertext documents accessible through any node in the network made the internet commercially viable.

The parallel for what some have described as the 'second' Internet is the original basis of the first Internet namely, creating an environment for computer science enthusiasts to develop time-sharing between users and subsequently rolling this out to wide area networks. By 1993, the internet was responsible for just 1% of the total telecommunications two-way information flow. By 2007 that number was 97%. Communication in the form of Instant messaging, video chat, VOIP, discussion forums, online shopping and more.

Forecasts of the internet going dark in the era of online video streaming (high density data) because of bottlenecking or systems being overwhelmed were written in the media. So far, that 'broken' internet phenomenon has not occurred. Yet with the advent of quantum computers, there is discussion about whether today's internet can handle the exploding data requirements, the facilitation of information flow and security considerations of quantum computers.

So, what might be the answer? The same impetus as the original Internet except for quantum. Creating an environment for quantum enthusiasts to develop time-sharing between users and subsequently rolling this out to wide area networks. Some combination of quantum networks, cloud configurations and ultimately a new quantum internet? The question becomes exponentially difficult when one considers, in the early stages of a technology (I'm old enough to recall the VHS vs Beta videotape rivalry) the numbers of types of quantum computers (we discuss many in this book) and how they and their systems will network together to communicate across buildings and across the globe.

If you're a business leader thinking about the value of quantum computing in 2021, you're probably looking at a complex problem that classical computers would take too long time to solve to make it viable for your company. Your team needs answers quickly derived to push out value to your customers and generate revenue. The same challenges over the history of entrepreneurial pursuits. As you'll see in Section 2, there are a myriad of applications being delivered and pursued today that could satisfy such needs. But what about communicating? Whether within or beyond your own company walls. Can you rely on today's internet? What if quantum cryptography advances faster than your company? What might that expose your company to in terms of email, data, customer information? Isn't all this an overwhelming set of challenges?

Yet it's important to go back to the fundamentals of quantum technology and the concept of entanglement. How two qubits can be entangled across great distances. A paper titled "Connecting Heterogeneous Quantum Networks by Hybrid Entanglement Swapping." in the May 29th, 2020 online issue of *Science Advances* is a case in point on how this scientific phenomenon could make quantum networks and the quantum internet a reality. The research forms a vital step toward the reality of "homogenous quantum networks." The authors from Kastler Brossel Laboratory (LKB) in Paris (Sorbonne Université, CNRS, ENS-Université PSL, Collège de France), with collaborators at NIST Boulder, asked the question whether different quantum platforms using different encoding could still communicate over a network.

So how will these quantum nodes communicate through a quantum system? Through non-classical correlations called entanglements which we discussed earlier. The LKB team stated "In quantum networks, the connection of distant nodes is performed by a specific operation called entanglement swapping. This procedure allows to connect systems that have never interacted before… {through]Bell-state measurement, effectively transfers—or "teleports"—the entanglement to the final systems."

The Major Components of a Quantum Network

Much like a classical network, a quantum network is composed of processors, nodes, fiber, switches and repeaters. Applications run on end nodes which are quantum processors incorporating a minimum of one qubit. To transport qubits between nodes, telecommunication fiber (light-based transmission) is used to link quantum processors of different wavelengths and hardware platforms. To maximize the use of telecommunication infrastructure, optical switches propel qubits to the destination processor to preserve quantum coherence. Quantum repeaters between nodes propel qubits over long distances and operate differently than classical repeaters since qubits cannot be copied.

The IBM Q Experience & Amazon Braket

In 2016, IBM began offering access to its quantum computer infrastructure through something they termed the IBM Quantum Experience (now The IBM Quantum Composer and the IBM Quantum Lab) being one of the first such services. By 2018, over 80,000 users had registered running collectively over 3 million experiments. In 2021, over 20 devices are available on the service, six of which are free to the public. IBM's quantum computers are of the superconducting variety operating within a dilution refrigerator with something called transmon qubits. Leveraging a quantum circuit model of computation, users create circuits using Qiskit and graphically with Quantum Composer or via programs in Quantum Lab Jupyter notebooks.

Amazon Web Services are well known in the computing world and with the addition of Amazon Braket (it's quantum computing service), users gain ready access to solving complex computational problems. Whether quantum research or HPC production workloads. Recently, Amazon added a new relationship to its offering. Clients can leverage the D-Wave Advantage System and 2000Q QPUs via Amazon Braket's Ocean plug-in. D-Wave's quantum annealing hardware is ideal for optimization computation problems, and D-Wave, as one of the first quantum startups (1999) has come a long way from its origins, offering clients practical advice and experience.

The Quantum Internet

Recently, the U.S. Department of Energy or DOE published a blueprint for a new internet with faster speeds, more security and capable of interacting through quantum networks. Starting in Chicago, DOE created a 52-mile-long quantum loop through its suburbs (the longest land-based QN in the world at the time).

A quantum internet would be a construct of linked quantum processors and networks Information flows in a quantum network through linked quantum processors (clusters) via entangled qubits which are inherently fragile. Distribution of a fragile resource like entanglement is thus inherently difficult between physically distant quantum processors and across whole systems yet the LKB team's work is an important step towards an eventual quantum internet.

Quantum internet applications, unlike their quantum computing cousins, require only modest quantum processors measuring a single qubit at a time. Quantum internet protocols including quantum key distribution for cryptography/security simpler processors preparing and measuring one qubit is required.

Quantum Superhighway...On Its Way?

Remember the "information superhighway" when the internet/World Wide Web started out? Well with recent developments in photonics and introducing silicon nitride (Si3N4) - significantly lower optical loss than silicon - combined with leveraging our global optical fibre network, we may be on the verge of the quantum superhighway. According to The Swiss Quantum Hub, "Encoding information into light, and transmitting it through optical fibers lies at the core of optical communications. With an incredibly low loss of 0.2 dB/km, optical fibers made from silica have laid the foundations of today's global telecommunication networks and our information society." Scientists at EPFL (École polytechnique fédérale de Lausanne) School of Basic Sciences have developed silicon nitride integrated circuits critical to the performance of photonic devices.

According to the US Department of Energy, which is driving the pursuit of the second Internet which would operate alongside the existing Internet, "a quantum Internet relies on photons exhibiting a quantum state known as entanglement, which allows them to share information over long distances without having a physical connection." Not only could a quantum internet (network of networks) enhance the flow of information, but because of the incredible difficulty in eavesdropping, information security is vastly improved as it passes between nodes…the unhackable internet. Part of the 2018 National Quantum Initiative Act, DOE scientists believe a prototype quantum communications system is possible before 2030.

Quantum networks (and a quantum internet) will require coherent photons streaming through fibre optic cables and a University in China has developed a new process in that direction. Coherent frequency conversion applies to communication, sensing, detecting and imaging applications.

The Second Internet or Quantum Internet thus may not be far off in the future. As companies prepare for a new method of communicating, understanding of the foundations of quantum computing and networking become more vital.

SECTION 2 Applied Quantum Computing

Use Cases for Today and Tomorrow

Chapter 10

Putting Quantum Computing to Work

'A lot of startups are founded by academics and have very little enterprise or entrepreneurial experience"
—William 'Whurley' Hurley,
Founder of Strangeworks Inc; Quantum Pioneer

Sitting at home during the pandemic, one's mind often wanders back to the days when you could get outside and engage in activities galore. Over my lifetime, mine were extreme sports including gliding, dog sledding, whitewater rafting, tree top climbing, and my ultimate favourite skydiving. Jumping into the world of quantum computing, for me, is the mental equivalent.

Anticipating my first skydive meant years of starts and stops, resulting in finally appearing at a small craft airport in Cookstown, Ontario, Canada. Fortunately, the day's sunshine and light wind conditions facilitated my attempt. After training (both reading and on-the-ground learning), we suited up, boarded the single-engine plane, rising to 12,500 feet in the air. At this point, while tipping out the plane with my tandem, I thought to myself "what are you doing?" but as I dropped to 6,000 feet and opened the parachute, I glided quietly through a nearby cloud, continuing ever-so-gently to the ground.

Experiencing the world of quantum computing (QC) mirrors that skydiving experience for me, but not physically, rather mentally. Having a career in business strategy, operations, process, credit, financial crimes, public speaking...nothing prepared me for the challenges of quantum physics. Still, like the end of the skydiving event, the feeling is incredibly satisfying. Concepts like entanglement and superposition, not native to a business mind, blew through my linear concept of science.

Four years later, the opportunities offered by quantum computing drive my motivation to learn more every day. Incredible programs from CERN and Delft University provided the theoretical foundations. Being the practical sort, I wanted to understand what quantum computing would be outside the research lab and academia. Reading about practical use cases for quantum computers was interesting, yet what was truly compelling was hearing about companies QC adventures from the pioneers themselves.

Quantum computing is now a global business with the largest organizations, like Google, Amazon, IBM, and Microsoft building solutions alongside companies making a real name for themselves in D-Wave Systems, IonQ, Rigetti and more. User organizations are plentiful as of 2020 knowing the technology is new and maturing daily. At conferences, the financial sector is regularly represented by Goldman Sachs, BBVA, and JP Morgan Chase. Automotive industry participants present include Volkswagen, BMW, and Ford. Aerospace companies Airbus and Boeing present as do pharmaceutical companies Biogen, Roche, and Takeda. The oil industry also understands the value of quantum computing with Exxon and British Petroleum presenting their real QC applications and strategies. Companies like Honeywell produce quantum computing capabilities both for their own internal needs as well as for clients, and the US Air

Force Research Laboratory is a leader in quantum pursuits for the US military.

Adding to the mix is a variety of quantum technology solutions (no market standard here yet - it's too 'early days') from quantum annealing to ion trap computers, from tens of qubits to thousands of them, from optimization specialty to molecular research uses, and from a variety of global teams generating new ideas daily.

So, how will mid and small-size companies (MSC) take advantage of quantum computing in the future. Will it simply be an off-the-shelf option? Will the quantum capability simply operate in the background? Will MSC leaders need to hire PhD's to take advantage of QC benefits? Will there be MSC-type business problems to solve leveraging this technology or is it only for large corporates (like the ones named above)?

These are important questions for MSC leaders to delve into, and sooner rather than later. One of the interesting opportunities I have is to read and review articles and posts about quantum computing. And there's no shortage of them in 2021. On a daily basis, I read at least five with truly new content - discoveries, dispelled myths, new applications, etc. So how can MSC leaders and their IT teams keep pace with a technology that may now be moving faster than AI? The future is uncertain and an adventure to be sure. And there are ways to navigate the morass of quantum information, travelling through the clouds and landing gently.

Akin to advanced technologies like artificial intelligence, it's critical for business leaders to remain focused on their business problems first rather than a shiny, new technology. Aligning the opportunities of quantum computing with those problems in priority order is paramount. Ensuring you have internal resources that can sustain the quantum solution once implemented is not a straightforward expectation yet again critical to success.

Try explaining to the CEO of a medium size business that you want him or her to invest in a technology based on the action and nature of energy and matter at the atomic and subatomic levels. Imagine the reaction. More likely the sales pitch will be what if we could conduct the same analysis on our most complex business problems in days or weeks instead of years (or seconds instead of days) with high accuracy and fidelity. Now they're listening. Sure there's a few caveats to those pronouncements but those details will get worked out right?

Just 5 years ago I was having the same conversations with business leaders about artificial intelligence. What's inside the black box they would ask? Why should I trust an unproven technology? Won't all our best people worry they'll be replaced by robots or computers linked to the cloud?

The Quantum for Business 2020 (or Q2B20) conference in December 2020, and the Quantum.Tech conference in April, 2021 reinforced for me the growing world of quantum computing applications to business. It confirmed my way of thinking about how I could convey the realities and complexities of quantum computing in a way that made sense to businesspeople. That not only were governments investing in quantum efforts, but so too was the corporate world.

My goal in this book is to leverage that experience, sharing the fundamental physics that makes quantum computing powerful and an interesting topic to study as well as its relationship to business success in the future. This book is intended for business and information technology leaders and participants who want to understand how this new incredible technology is expected to impact their department, company, industry, strategic choices, and future.

What the World Knows About Quantum

Yet how many people in the world understand quantum computing? Let's start with a subject much older - Calculus. The total number of book titles on Amazon (which owns over 80% of the publishing market) is 57 million covering all topics. Of those, there are only 60,000 titles associated with calculus, or about 0.1%. Quantum computing has just 2,000 titles on Amazon and 1/10 of the searches for calculus on Google. So, simply based on the number of titles available and searches, the relative population learning about quantum computing today remains a miniscule fraction of the world. OMDIA, a tech research firm, conducted a survey of hundreds of business leaders in 2021 asking about their QC investment plans. 80% had yet to start, were evolving rudimentary plans or investigating initial use cases. Only 2% of survey respondents had an existing plan to deploy, while none yet had plans to scale across multiple units.

Today's written word covering quantum computing speaks most often to the underlying quantum mechanics, physics, algorithm development, and hardware. Yet little has been written about how businesses can leverage such a futuristic, advanced technology in real business applications. I hope to inspire the reader to look outside their industry and IT departments' current focus to gain at least a surface understanding of quantum computing and some of the applications in current day use and the possible opportunities in the future.

Earlier, I referenced Robert Schoekopf's, quote, "If you had brought an iPhone to someone 25 years ago, they would have called you a wizard." In 2021, the same applies to quantum computing technology. It seems too futuristic to be practical. When business leaders have so many competing priorities, how can one add such an unknown quantity to the mix?

So as a business leader, that has done some reading, you would know there is a world of opportunity in quantum computing. Yet, how much do you need to know about the complex topic? Do you need to take dozens of courses, interview dozens of vendors, ramp up on internal talent? When quantum computing is so complex and changing so frequently, and so few are investing today, how will you know when your organization is and should be quantum ready?

Before Artificial Intelligence became somewhat mainstream, I often encountered business leaders who would first ask not “how can we use AI?” but “what is AI?” So, we were starting from ground zero in introducing AI to the business. Within a few years, as more recognizable commodities or services like GPS’ and Netflix became powered by artificial intelligence more business leaders began asking the “how can we use AI?” question.

As a career banker turned Artificial Intelligence strategist, I felt confident in my own knowledge about AI, yet what became abundantly clear was that to solve the world's truly big problems, and exploding amounts of data, an alternative to traditional computing was needed. Climate change, healthcare, and the world of finance share a common bond - billions of bits of information that need to be analyzed for patterns and options through scenarios that would take tens, even hundreds of years for traditional computing to solve. So my pursuits a few years ago routed me towards the field of quantum computing.

Imagine this option as a business or organization leader. Rather than approaching scenario analysis in a linear fashion, one could look at all scenarios simultaneously. All combinations of molecules to result in one scenario with the highest probability of successfully achieving one's objectives in the time it would take to calculate just one on today's traditional hardware. While I may be oversimplifying based on the current state of quantum computing in 2020, organizations need to start looking at this capability today to plan for their future.

Today, in 2021, the majority of business leaders would be at the stage of asking the question “what is quantum computing?”, yet it won’t take years for the follow-up of how to use quantum computing given the groundswell of QC activity happening globally. The media is barraging the internet with articles on breakthroughs and examples of partnerships making practical use of quantum computing.

Take the Glaxo Smith Kline and D-Wave Systems partnership on optimizing protein folding. Or IQM's partnership with Atos (France) and CSC (Finland) to accelerate the commercialization of European quantum technologies. Or the "successful field trial of quantum-secured transport in Germany using ADVA's encryption with IDQ's Quantum Key Distribution". Healthcare, diverse tech, quantum cryptography – all these fields of quantum endeavor are brimming with activity by quantum innovation. So, business leaders take notice. If you aren't studying quantum computing for your business, incorporating it into your strategy and finding talented resources to fulfill your strategy, your competitors likely are.

The, CEO of Zapata Computing, Christopher Savoie once articulated that quantum computing was rapidly drawing near to a turning point at which quantum computing would begin generating tangible business value not available from classical computing. "IBM, Google, Honeywell, Rigetti, IonQ and others are all creating increasingly powerful quantum devices…In the near term, these devices are noisy and prone to error, but the right software can correct for these errors and unlock applications," argues Savoie.

I recently attended the Quantum Tech 2021 Conference with 1,800 other quantum experts and enthusiasts. Speakers from around the globe in aerospace, automotive, computing, consulting, technology and other industries converged on the conference. What surprised me most was the balanced approach they were taking. As excited as they were about the prospects of quantum computing, they talked about the hype, about the need to ensure QC was the right solution for their business problem, and about possible quantum "winters" where investment could dry up without significant results.

The Business Leaders' Quantum Formula

If you don't have a background in quantum computing, yet you run an organization that might benefit from the technology, what do you do. Is there a formula? Well, it may not be as simple as y=f(x). Such a formula might not resemble Schrodinger's equation (you might have heard of the experiment with a cat inside the box being both dead and alive until we open the box akin to our hamburger/hotdog example). The leadership formula, equation or algorithm need not be so complex.

In my practice, I work with scaling companies who want to insert advanced technology into their business without upsetting core operations and core revenues. I take each leader through an opportunity assessment that offers a holistic look without an extended timeframe. In fact, in the span of four meetings over an equal number of weeks, we develop a robust strategy with prioritized timelines, supporting research and a renewed confidence in how to proceed.

Earlier this year, I embarked on a consulting engagement with four scaling companies in Canada. Each had either identified a use case or were open to leveraging artificial intelligence within their business, resulting in use cases or applications that were both customer-facing and operational. I introduced each to my companies' proprietary Artificial Intelligence Opportunity Assessment incorporating matrices, questions, and graphics driving both a broad understanding of the opportunities and a narrowing of their priorities. The outcome? Some AI would be "built" or developed in-house, while in other cases partners or vendors would be approached. Because of the exercise, all these companies are better positioned to integrate AI now and in the future. One founder commented that the process "has helped us define a strategy where we can apply practical AI technology to solve some near-term tactical needs and over time extend our use to create a significant competitive differentiator."

For one of these clients, we began looking out a couple of years from now, post-implementing a series of AI tactics, into leveraging quantum computing (QC). The use cases? Natural Language processing (or NLP). So, the conversation led us into the question of, if you start down the path, would you "buy, build or borrow" when it came to QC? Simple, one might say, at this stage of quantum computing maturity. Surely many would argue to not "build" when one combines the relatively immature or unproven technology and the cost to develop one's own. This book is devoted to those organizational leaders and managers entering the world of quantum computing, for the first time, or those seeking to dig deeper with some early level of insight into this relatively new technology. To map out their unique quantum path, organizations need to consider a series of questions, and we articulate some of those questions (by no means all given space limitations and overwhelming our readers).

Organizational leaders view technologies like quantum computing very differently. Some ponder quantum mobilization options. They might look at QC as a way to disrupt their industry, charging their teams to experiment with quantum solutions internally. Others may push such efforts to expert groups outside the organization. Still others are simply skeptics of the technology (akin to the maturity stages we explored earlier). In terms of the speed of adoption, some organizational leaders see technology as overly hyped by the media or believe there does not exist a sufficient depth of understanding of the technology within their companies to pursue. Finally, some leaders will demand to understand the policy spectrum including government programs or ecosystems, current strength of education systems, and the issue of constraints in place to get a system confidence level like fault tolerant quantum computers.

Buy, Build or Borrow

The answer to the "buy, build or borrow" decision of course is "it depends". The vendor market for quantum hardware and software is growing yet limited in 2021. Quantum hardware vendors (IBM, Rigetti, D-Wave, Honeywell, Google, Microsoft, AWS, etc.) with viable solutions do exist. So, why would a commercial entity attempt to build their own multi-million-dollar quantum computer when several viable options already exist? Where will you invest internally versus externally to be "quantum ready". Can you ignore the build option and rely on Quantum-as-a-Service at this stage of your quantum readiness?

If the decision is to build some of the technology in-house, (predominantly software), there are a number of steps to follow in order to achieve increasing levels of readiness. Core to the exercise is identifying the business need and whether that need aligns with internal priorities and goals whether at a unit or enterprise level. Next, illustrating alignment with customer /user needs and financial viability would take place. Documenting the forgoing through a business case, gaining approval, testing and validation follow.

Once you have journeyed through all these issues of value, you need to amplify the probability of success by considering various vectors in the intense series of quantum questions. The questions surrounding the development of a quantum computing strategy for any business are numerous. In this section we review the "buy, borrow, build" decisions that organizational leaders will need to undertake as the quantum computing era evolves and accelerates. "Buy" refers to the purchase of quantum hardware, software or services (QHSS). "Borrow" refers to licensing schemes or alliances. "Build" refers to the internal development of some part of the QHSS tech stack.

In building or crafting the algorithm, at the foundation, basic research should include a conceptual framework for quantum algorithms (QA), followed by formulation and testing. A proof of concept is then constructed, followed by a small-scale test illustrating how the quantum algorithm performs better than classical algorithms.

Should the organization achieve the foundational level, then incorporating the QA into a prototype application (with an appropriate interface, classical or otherwise). Using test cases that are representative, the team would need to demonstrate the performance of the application over classical code. Finally, the team would need to illustrate the scalability of the algorithm and application beyond the initial test cases.

Is 2021 the right time to build a quantum computing full-stack solution in-house? Is it even feasible? Is your organization ready for a quantum computing ecosystem? Have you developed a short, medium and long-term quantum computing strategy? Do you have the right talent on-board? How about trusted partners to deliver on your strategy? Do you have a complex business problem that aligns with current quantum capabilities like optimization? Can you integrate the results of the solution into an action for the business i.e. Is it useful? Does it survive a rigorous cost-benefit analysis?

Preparing for the future of a relatively new technology can be a challenge. The Head of the Quantum Science Program at Fermilab, Panagiotis Spentzouris, said “We are entering a very exciting era for quantum computing, with quantum computers moving from the academic lab to being deployed and available through the cloud … there is a lot of pressure to demonstrate impactful applications in the short term. My advice to anyone starting now is to balance the needs for long term development to those of quick demonstrators, stay focused on the ultimate goal of delivering an error corrected quantum computer, and, most importantly, enjoy the journey. It is going to be very exciting for the next dėcade-plus!”

The statistics presented in Section 1 of this book illustrate, if you're at all uncertain, about whether this technology has a practical future. So many quantum use cases and applications are already underway. Yet do you have to go it alone? Can your leadership team comfortably make these decisions today or do you need help navigating the relatively new technology field? Can you maintain and run the purchased infrastructure? Is this a specific business problem/one-off where a partnership or vendor arrangement is more appropriate? Or is this a design program that operates continually in the business and needs QC to be in-house to protect proprietary work?

These are merely a fraction of the questions associated with the 'quantum ready' decision. If you're leading an organization that is ripe with quantum computing talent (a rarity today) you may be open to enveloping more of the quantum tech stack internally. If you are simply opening the door to QC, connecting with an objective source like the Quantum Computing Report or a local meetup community is a better starting point. If you are somewhere in between, reflect on the questions I posed earlier and connect with the publisher of this book about our Quantum Computing Opportunity Assessment.

If you're like most companies, you're most likely to focus on Quantum-as-a-service incorporating the various elements above in a third-party full stack solution fueled by your company's data, but these questions will collectively more closely guide your "buy, build or borrow" decision. Organizations have much to consider in the quantum computing world, yet a structured approach should enhance your probabilities of success.

How to Demonstrate Value

Solve problems that are not solvable with classical computers.

C-suite leaders may look at quantum computers as merely another tool. When making the quantum investment recommendation, the resounding question will likely be, "Can't we do this with our existing computers or software upgrades?" Unless the answer is a firm no, then executives will tend to stick with the tried and true. Be clear on the difference. Ensure your team understands the problems and potential options well enough to have a direct line of sight to the quantum option. As Bob Sutor, VP at IBM says, "Don't do quantum simply for quantum's sake."

Determine 'value for whom'

Who is the value directed towards? Is it the research scientists who are experimenting with new molecule combinations or portfolio optimization models? Or is the value for customers who will benefit from new healthcare or security solutions? Or is the executive group who can loudly pronounce their technology leadership, brand promotion, or financial stakeholder benefits? C-suite people often don't provide a charter for quantum computing (or for any other new technology for that matter) so clarity of value becomes critical to gain acceptance.

Identify the type(s) of value

Is the primary value impact on profits and losses? Or maybe it's technical performance in solving a research or optimization problem faster and more accurately. Is this a Euro's or dollar's value that is clearly identifiable – money certainly talks. Is this about disrupting the value chain and taking a competitive lead in your industry? Maybe there's a 10x or 100x improvement in some metric as a result of introducing quantum computing. Or in some instances, it's about a step change, where you did not have a way to solve the problem before and now you do.

Alignment to Organizational Values

Your quantum computing ideas will get nowhere unless they are tied to the organization's key priorities and goals. If this is a pet project, with a team who is excited about a new technology – full stop. On the other hand, if you've done your homework and there is alignment, you're on to the next step.

Engaging Others

Champions with influence in an organization are your first and possibly most important audience. There are examples of grass roots evolution of quantum computing within some entities, however the more traditional path is through senior leaders who understand and will champion your quantum initiative. Also, look across industries, meetups and networks for successful quantum projects and precedents.

Roadmap the Value

People love to be able to envision the future and a roadmap is an excellent way to do that. Showing peers or management that the vision is to invest in quantum computing over a period of years while reaping the benefits in the short term and how that's going to happen (beyond just an elevator speech) will help you start on the road to your quantum goals sooner. Your roadmap should include the four phases namely discovery (which problems and are they the right ones for QC), math (mapping the algorithms, pilots (doing field tests) and production. Some experts suggest the first three phases could take 6-12 months, so moving production to value needs to start along the roadmap as soon as practical.

The Human Factor

Yet what about the people in your organization – the individual businessperson or professional? How does one prepare for the 'Age of Quantum Computing'? When so few people understand what quantum computing means (is entanglement and superposition part of your everyday language?), how can they understand the implications of the new technology?

Consider the people evolution impact of AI. Today's workforce is reeling from the impact of technologies like artificial intelligence. Whether it's speed of progress, privacy issues, ethical use, or Terminator-type predictions, AI's benefits and risks continue to be explored and certainly remain only partially known. Job candidates must deal with robot resume filters and interviewers. Radiologists compete with AI-powered systems with greater and greater precision and reliability. Yoga instructors either augment their practice or compete with tools that hyper-accurately analyse their clients' movements and recommend improvements. Prognosticators have predicted for years that there will be millions of job losses while others suggest AI will augment existing jobs (much like previous industrial revolutions have resulted in more net new jobs).

Then along comes quantum computing or QC. A technology based on the smallest particles of our universe—atoms, photons and electrons—and the way they interact creating vast new ways to compute. So, if you are one of the billions of people in today's workforce or soon to be entering it, do you need to worry? Or is this technology merely in the realm of academia or the laboratory? How can business leaders achieve a reasonable level of comprehension on such a complex subject? While the timing of commercialized quantum computing may be in question, the eventuality is not.

With every industrial revolution, humans have leveraged the newly available technology to pursue and solve new problems. So too with quantum computing. And human interaction will not fade, thus requiring people to continue to interact with others. Healthcare jobs, for example, are exploding around the world (occupations "according to the US Dept of Labor) even as technology takes new leaps.

As with AI, being creative and innovative is as important as the tools with which to explore opportunities and challenges. Those are human elements. Dr. Jaclyn Lee of Singapore University of Technology and Design (SUTD) describes the future of jobs in her 2020 book "Accelerating Organisation Culture Change Through Digital Tools". She contends "…more jobs will move from physical manual labor to work that is creative and innovative" and goes further to predict that "skills that will be in demand will be the ability to work across disciplines, being creative and innovative, and possessing good communication and people skills." In that vein, instinct, judgment and empathy are vital skills or capabilities yet to be replicated by advanced technology. So the employee of the future needs to leverage humanity and advanced technology in combination.

Boeing executive Jay Lowell, Chief Engineer, Disruptive Computing and Networks, believes that it's not enough to be simply an expert in quantum computing. You need something else – another skill set or two – to bring to the team. In Boeing's case that might be mechanical or electrical engineering. In other businesses it might be some other domain knowledge. And learners need to be quick at understanding and adapting to the science of quantum computing. Project groups need a spectrum of individuals. In fact, at Boeing in the Disruptive Computing and Networks team, quantum-types are in the minority, reflecting the belief that team members can be trained to learn the quantum component.

Getting the Team Quantum Ready

One of the leading voices in quantum today is Carl Williams, Deputy Director of the National Institute of Standards and Technology (NIST) Physical Measurement Laboratory (PML). He has been involved in the technology world for decades and understands the dynamics impacting the quantum evolution. According to Mr. Williams, "what I learned, way back in 2002, is that when that ship leaves port, you have to have a team who understood the technology and understood your business model. You have to have both of those together — technology and business model — to see if this will affect your bottom line."

According to numerous sources, there is a serious lack of non-technical talent in the quantum workforce. People with functional backgrounds like operations, marketing, HR and sales who have gained insight into quantum technology offer good value to quantum companies rich in technical talent, yet lacking in establishing or driving a business forward.

The Advanced Technology Academic Research Center or ATARC, headquartered in Virginia, hosted a session covering quantum's future impact. The 2021 session covered many fields including how use cases like multi-vehicle routing problems can be applied to people, assets, vaccine and other distribution optimization challenges with a demo by D-Wave Systems Inc. Representative Jim Langevin (US) attended the meeting and reaffirmed the importance of a sustained quantum literacy investment in people talent going forward. The head of the Quantum Economic Development Consortium (QEDC) – whose mission is to "grow a robust commercial quantum-based industry and associated supply chain in the United States" concurred that a diverse talent mix is needed and that the challenge is a global one.

I attended a presentation by the UK Quantum Simulation and Computing Hub (17 Universities and 25+ Commercial Partners) titled “Quantum Computing & a Diverse Workforce” discussing their organization's focus on equality, diversity and inclusion and the UK quantum ecosystem. What struck me was the myriad of factors the organization had to consider in managing such a workforce in the 2020’s. Then add in quantum skills and crossover to business demands.

IBM suggests that “building a quantum workforce requires interdisciplinary education and the promise of real jobs”. IBM states there’s a five-step process: Designating knowledgeable employees as “quantum champions”, identifying use cases, experimenting with solutions for actual problems, creating a roadmap for next steps, and embracing flexibility because the technology is rapidly evolving.

Does every employee of the future need to be a PhD? Does one need to have started to learn about QC at an early age? Can one learn at least something about the field from YouTube or free education platforms like edX? The answers are no, no and yes. I am avid user of both of YouTube and edX platforms to learn about advanced technology including QC, each time learning about a new research development or use case at no extra cost.

Developers should apply their efforts in the real world, trying the IBM Quantum Lab where one can get “cloud access to the most advanced quantum computers available…to learn, develop, and run programs.” Your programs. Or Microsoft’s Quantum Development Kit samples. The options are significantly vaster than just a few years ago.

The Approach to Innovation

In 2021, one might imagine that companies all over the world are charging down the door to innovate given the preponderance of new technologies at their disposal. That seems not to be the case, however. Boston Consulting Group's "Most Innovative

Companies 2021: Overcoming the Innovation Readiness Gap", determined while 75% of companies are making innovation (a top three priority), only 20% self-declared being fully ready to deliver the innovation they argued was crucial to their organizational performance.

Certainly the pandemic has forced organizations to rethink their strategies for the future, pivoting in some cases into whole new businesses. Innovation in service, product, and technology are now high on the list of organizational priorities and quantum computing should be considered within such strategies when the business problems align.

BCG contends that the top innovation companies exhibit innovation ambition, governance, culture and domains while ensuring their ideas fit with the marketplace, performance management and internal ecosystems. Some of their top 10 include quantum computing vendors like Alphabet (Google), Amazon, Microsoft and IBM, yet a company does need to be 'Big Tech' any longer to benefit from quantum computing within their innovation strategy, though it's better if you have some key people to lead that effort.

The CIO Role & Quantum

Forbes' 2021 Top 50 Innovative Technology Leaders list includes CIO's from a broad range of industries. As a CIO in this era, staying on top of technological evolution is a greater challenge than ever. Forbes says compiling the list highlights "how the CIO role has evolved from its traditional focus on serving other corporate functions to one that emphasizes broad innovation and collaboration. Technology leaders are using data and machine intelligence to help identify new business opportunities and then co-creating products and services with their C-suite peers to take advantage of these." Not only have CIO's had to deal with the impact of the pandemic (think work-from-anywhere and e-commerce tech solutions) on their organizations, but also with the challenge of making key decisions with limited budgets on a technology that is yet to proven on a widespread basis, like quantum computing.

CIO's recruit and engage talent within their organizations to fill skills, knowledge and operational gaps, yet when it comes to quantum, supply is scarce. Universities are only gradually establishing programs, other than those at a PhD level which have been around for years. Companies must work with vendors pending an in-house solution, if at all. New roles emerge as technology evolves. It happened in the last decade with artificial intelligence and machine learning. It will happen with quantum computing. Yet before a CIO goes about hiring an army of data scientists (like many organizations have done), they may want to consider a different role to start their quantum journey.

The Quantum Business Strategist

Organizations need to start considering the value of quantum technology and the talent they need to populate their teams. With billions of dollars being invested globally both publicly and privately, industry players racing to new discoveries and solutions, and prospective clients desperately trying to understand the potential for their organizations, never before has there been a greater need for the Quantum Business Strategist.

The Quantum Business Strategist (QBS) represents a fundamentally new way to address quantum technology implementation and evolution within organizations. The quantum 'quarterback' (the QBS) leads the discussion between C-Suite and IT leaders in organizations and as an external consultant with client companies.

Requiring a broad set of skills and knowledge, the QBS should have deep business acumen, some knowledge of quantum physics and mechanics, and insights into the global quantum ecosystem (its' players, its' trends, its' cost structure, its' options, and more). The QBS need not be a PhD, or lifelong quantum technology industry participant. Organizations, whether government, industry or academia, consistently argue they need talent with sales, marketing, and operational experience as well as quantum knowledge, insight and experience and the QBS role is ideally suited for these challenges.

Inspiring long-run organizational quantum success, the QBS supports the development of a quantum mission, vision, goals, strategies, KPI's and tactics for the organization in near, mid and long-term. By staging quantum activities within the organization, its' leaders (at various hierarchical levels) and employees acclimatize themselves to this complex, relatively immature technology, its myriad of options, and permit investment decisions to be prioritized alongside business goals.

Leveraging quantum opportunity assessments, (QA), quantum implementation templates (QIT), and quantum strategy roadmaps (QSR), the Quantum Business Strategist must have a business and customer-first approach to the technology. Quantum computing provides great potential, yet must be appropriately aligned with the goals of the business (not simply a shiny new piece of tech). Through analysis of the QA and QIT, leadership, employee and customer input, and industry insights, the QBS can develop a roadmap to enhance the success potential of quantum technology within an organization. Through the QBS' roadmap, organizations gain greater comfort combatting concerns of falling behind the competition, or behind a rapidly advancing technology. Providing resources, outside industry use cases, vendor contacts, and common-language recommendations, the QBS offers leadership a valuable quantum industry professional.

New roles are being created daily in the world of quantum computing. Quantum hardware engineers, quantum algorithm developers, quantum full stack developer are roles that appear on

Indeed and other recruiting sites regularly now. The role of Quantum Business Strategist will soon join these other functions in their contribution to a successful quantum implementation and roadmap.

Learning Opportunities

Just as quantum computing brings a whole new set of business opportunities, the field has its own language and ways of operating. Many online courses about quantum computing recommend a basic familiarity with linear algebra. As Microsoft describes it in its Quantum Documentation, "Linear algebra is the language of quantum computing." Researchers and developers use linear algebra to describe qubit states and quantum operations as well as to predict what a quantum computer will do in response to a set of instructions.

So, how do you start? Veronica Combs, senior writer at TechRepublic wrote in *Innovation* on November 23, 2020, said "The first step is to understand qubits and superposition. The next one is to get a handle on the business advantage that this technology represents."

John Preskill, Director of the Institute for Quantum Information and Matter at Caltech and Amazon Scholar argues "For the best preparation, get a broad education, covering physical science, computer science, and engineering, so you can understand the full stack from hardware to applications."

Arvind Krishna, CEO of IBM once said "Quantum computing must also be ubiquitous in the classroom. From computer science courses to chemistry and business classes, today's students need to understand the technology, and hopefully pursue career paths routed in quantum computing." This may seem like an astounding pronouncement, yet the maturity of the technology is picking up steam and it will become increasingly easy for businesses to fall behind. Another

IBM'er, Jay Gambetta, Vice President of Quantum Computing suggests "Learn lots of background. No area is off limits, as quantum touches many different things. Getting experience is key."

If you're a scientist and considering the world of quantum computing as your next endeavor, University of Waterloo's Quantum Information Graduate program may be for you billing itself as it "prepares students not only to participate in this quantum revolution, but to lead it." CERN's quantum computing course offered me first-hand access to one of the world's quantum thought leaders in Elias Fernando Combarro-Alvarez; a course I suggest readers investigate. MIT's xPro Quantum Computing Fundamentals comes highly recommended by a recent graduate and colleague Esperanza Cuenca Gomez of Madrid, Spain. Or plan on digging into tutorials and lab tours from companies like D-Wave.

CERN Course

If you're considering learning quantum computing, algorithms and programming there are several great places to get started namely IBM, CERN, D-Wave, Quantum meetups amongst many others. For six consecutive weeks, I attended Friday morning sessions (to be clear attending live meant 4:30 am Eastern Time) offered by CERN and hosted by Elias Fernandez-Combarro Alvarez, an associate professor in the Computer Science Department at the University of Oviedo in Spain since 2009 and a cooperation associate at CERN since earlier this year.

I was looking for a way to learn about Quantum Computing, not just through reading articles or books or watching YouTube videos or investing in a class I wasn't ready to. CERN's Online Introductory Lectures on Quantum Computing were ideal for my needs. And for many others apparently as well. Alberto Di

Meglio, the openlab head at CERN recently said "just because someone knows physics doesn't mean they can use quantum out of the box....It took us by surprise that the first lecture was followed by almost 2,000 people around the world."

Host Fernandez- Combarro Alvarez's confident, calm approach to the subjects of quantum communication protocols, linear algebra, rotation, super dense coding and more have made it easier for this "practical" strategist in AI to understand the basics, the basis and the potential of quantum technology.

Coding training programs are offered increasingly to our children. Coding helps children understand another language and the computing world around them - for every letter, number, phrase or instruction, there's a combination of 1's and 0's in code that drives computing. Coding cultivates creativity through experimentation, making mistakes, testing and adjusting. Coding enhances math skills by applying math to practical things like game development. By learning how to organize their thoughts, young minds can achieve better writing skills over time. Finally, coding can improve problem solving ability through trying one route, observing the outcome, and if that route doesn't work then they can try to solve the problem in another way.

Learning about quantum computing should be a multi-faceted endeavor. Academic institutions, real-world experience, periodical sources like Medium.com, the Quantum Computing Report, The Quantum Daily and connecting with quantum leaders are excellent ways for the workforce of the future to prepare.

My favourite sources for learning more about quantum computing? I get information pushed to me from periodicals like Swiss Quantum Hub, The Quantum Daily, the Quantum Computing Report, the Quantum News, phys.org, Science Tech Daily and Medium.com articles and Google updates. In the span of just 12 months, I've collected over 500 unique articles about QC and QC breakthroughs. I'm avidly curious. If you're on the edges of quantum computing, as a leader or employee, these periodicals can provide the insights into this field that you need.

If you're a quantum rookie, meetups are a great way to meet others interested in speaking, presenting and merely being curious about the field of quantum computing. Over 17,000 people in 74 quantum meetup communities in 55 cities from 20 different countries are connecting today.

When on a quest to do some testing on quantum computers, you're not looking to go online or go to a computer retailer in the quantum world. The reality is much more virtual. Individual users leverage their own laptops through the cloud to access quantum computing time on manufacturers sites. Commercially accessible quantum computing from vendors like Microsoft, IBM and AWS makes more sense today through a relatively few pieces of hardware as opposed to selling many quantum computers separately. As time passes, the quantum laptop may change that view, though that is years away.

The advantage of the IBM Quantum Lab and Qiskit exists in the opportunity for users of all skills and backgrounds to experiment with quantum computing by designing quantum circuits through a drag and drop interface. Leveraging different numbers of qubits and applying logic gates, users can understand how they impact the state vectors of qubits. IBM's Qiskit (a python library permitting users to play with popular quantum algorithms) can be used inside IBM Q in a Jupyter notebook to implement Shor's algorithms among others.

Quantum Conferences

One thing there is no shortage of today is quantum related conferences and they are readily found. For readers interested in checking out upcoming conferences, you might start with

Quantum Computing Report with its list of a variety of conferences. Waget.org provides a list of over 300 conferences in 2021 mostly dedicated to academia and researchers. IEEE organizes their own conferences including IEEE Quantum Week usually in October of the year. Quantum Flagship has a broad diversity of hackathons, workshops and symposiums. Q2B2020 (hosted by QCWare) focused on the business side of quantum and Quantum.Tech's conference is attended by over 1500 quantum experts and enthusiasts. Check out our Notes section for this chapter for links to those groups.

Conclusion

Roles within our workforce are changing. The "quantum engineer" is not a futuristic position, rather one of today. Equally important is the quantum storyteller, the person who can bridge organizational needs with quantum capabilities. The quantum business strategist is a new but vital role. Understanding traditional computing and combining that capability with newer methods to achieve an organizations performance goals is rare in the AI ecosystem let alone the quantum universe. Striving to be that bridge would be a useful target for those interested in quantum computing today or in the future.

As we asked earlier, do you need to be a PhD to understand quantum computing, its challenges and opportunities? Not at all. Yet like artificial intelligence, the quantum workforce will need to devote time to comprehending the technology and working with teams of skilled, creative people to solve some of our world's most complex and urgent problems.

We've offered up a long list of learning and doing opportunities. In 2021, the list is longer than ever, and will continue to grow. It's an exciting time and I wish those who are or will become part of the quantum workforce a wonderful journey.

I have a highly practical nature, and enjoy seeing ideas put in motion. When quantum computing hit my radar, I quickly realized what the future might hold - converging technologies being applied to numerous challenges in every industry. Artificial intelligence, 5G, DNA data storage capabilities, and quantum computing converging to address the biggest problems being experienced by humans including climate change, security, hunger, carbon footprint/self-driving electric vehicles and covid-19 research, road asset management and manufacturing. Use cases for quantum computing that are not years away. Each are current demands for a transformational technology being fast-tracked by an increasing number of researchers and vendors. The technology field is ripe for quantum developments and business should be ready to take advantage of quantum capabilities including the next generation of quantum internet, quantum phase batteries and quantum superconductors to name a few.

Chapter 11

Quantum-Powered Decision Making

"Doing is a quantum leap from imagining" – Barbara Sher, speaker, career coach and author.

How many decisions do you make on any given day? Decisions about when to trade an investment, what errands you will do that day, what to eat or a myriad of others. Similarly, for organizations, billions of decisions, with a preponderance of factors, are made daily about staffing, investments, and operations. To address such quantities and complexities, is there a role for quantum computers in the decision-making process?

What is Decision-making? *Decision-making formalizes how one specific agent should take an action in the context of unknown probabilistic environments to optimize the reward of the decision. Each action option presented to the agent offers different probabilities of success or completion and potentially different rewards or penalties.*

What Constitutes Effective Decision-making?

Below are 12 characteristics of effective decision-making derived from a variety of public and private sources:

- Well defined problem
- Clear criteria for selecting best option including reasonable probabilities

- Accurate data
- Many alternatives
- Permits replicability
- Includes many voices
- Provides executable decisions
- Solutions are feasible
- Is systematic (structured set of steps)
- Recognise & filter blind spots including team's own cognitive bias
- Speed
- Decisions can be evaluated and monitored

It's never easy to apply all 12 factors but let's first take a math-oriented approach. The effective decision, based on the above 12 factors, for the 'mathies' amongst our readers, could be represented as: y1 (decision) = f (x1, x2, x3, x4...x12) and the probability of y1 being considered effective is based on the weightings (importance and/or probability of achieving the factor) or w1, w2...w12 being in place or Prob (y1 decision) =f (x1 w1, x2 w2, ...x12 w12). So, could an effective decision formula move from an equation into an algorithm, either classical or quantum? Could a quantum computer generate millions of options, probabilities of success and highly accurate predictions of outcomes, either reward or penalties?

The 'robot in the maze' problem is a simplified view of this where in the classical domain, the robot studies each move sequentially, whereas in the quantum domain, the robot studies all possible moves at once to reach the destination. The robots' decisions are either classical or quantum. An effective decision is impacted by the ability to analyse many steps quickly to reach the maze's exit in the quickest manner, with the least energy expenditure.

In the 'travelling salesperson' example, the salesperson wants to optimize the route between many cities to decide how to travel that day with the least amount of cost and time and optimal results. Company A wants to send a salesperson from its head office to 14 separate cities in the optimal path. Today's best computers can perform that operation in seconds. Yet, increasing the number to 22 cities with the same laptop and algorithm could take 2,000 years. Here is where quantum computing becomes invaluable since, for every additional city, the computing power required balloons. Really? Yes. For example, 11 cities translate to 20 million routes between them, 12 cities — 240 million routes and 15 cities — more than 650 billion. For a quantum computer, the effort associated with additional cities does not substantially increase the compute requirement. Extend this example to an airline where one would add equipment readiness, passenger preferences, weather, and numerous other factors to become an optimization nightmare. But not necessarily for a quantum computer.

What Role Can QC Play in Decision-making?

If you have traveled beyond the concept that "quantum computing is mostly hype", and accept the applications arriving into the ecosystem today, is it conceivable decision-making, like optimization for example, can benefit from quantum computing?

In late 2020, IBM held a three-week challenge where participants used a Grover's algorithm-based design game and quantum random access memory or qRAM to learn about implementing complex quantum data structures. Participants recognized through the exercise that the combination could solve real-life, complex decision-making problems.

There is also another approach. By modelling the human brain, our languages, our memory, and other factors, quantum experts have asserted a concept called quantum cognition which is "based on various cognitive phenomena defined by the quantum theory of information to describe the process of decision making using of quantum probabilities. "Several recent studies have intersected human electromechnical processes with how a quantum representation of "uncertainty in generation of action potentials" applying quantum cognition to real life decisions.

The Practice of Quantum-Powered Decision-Making

Now let's turn to several use cases for quantum computing in decision-making, namely financial trading, autonomous vehicles, the legal field and regulation.

Financial Trading

Financial services altered in 2015 with the advent of fintech companies – smaller entities automating traditional banking tasks like credit analysis and payments. With quantum computing, financial services is evolving again. Fraud detection, one of my former financial services careers, and portfolio risk optimization using quantum computing changes the playing field forever. By taking into consideration thousands of factors, quantum computing methodologies are expected to readily identify key fraud indicators. By identifying key interdependencies, more attractive, lower risk investment portfolios become possible. Companies like JP Morgan Chase, Barclay's, Commonwealth Bank and Goldman Sachs use quantum computing for portfolio optimization, trading strategies, market simulations, risk analysis, asset pricing and fraud detection.

The President of Honeywell Quantum Solutions, Tony Uttley, argued in 2020 that "One of the areas being looked at currently is in the area of artificial intelligence within financial trading. Quantum physics is probabilistic, meaning the outcomes constitute a predicted distribution. In certain classes of problems, where outcomes are governed by unintuitive and surprising relationships among the different input factors, quantum computers have the potential to better predict that distribution thereby leading to a more correct answer."

McKinsey & Company, the global consulting firm, agrees in that given financial services companies operate in a world of abundant structured and unstructured data, they will need more powerful computers to process that data, calculating more accurate probabilities at faster speeds than in the past to remain competitive. With more reliable and detailed insights, banks, for example, can make better decisions regarding capital market trades, more relevant offers, more precise credit exposure analysis along with better portfolio management and more personalized customer service.

Automotive & Robot Navigation Decisions

Imagine if you will city streets with no traffic signals or stop signs. And no accidents. If autonomous vehicles (AV) achieve the hopes and expectations of AV manufacturers, then such a sight could be a reality. With every AV not only monitoring its own activities but communicating with every other relevant vehicle, making real-time decisions, not only will image recognition, LIDAR/RADAR, and other capabilities be required, but also the computing power of quantum computers. Smart cities will combine artificial intelligence with quantum computing to define patterns of virtually any kind from large complex datasets.

Over the years, Boston Dynamics' Atlas robot progressed from unstable approaches to a set of stairs to the equivalent of human parcours and dancing by leveraging ever more sophisticated machine learning. The device autonomously vacuuming your carpets demonstrated progression over time, where they now continuously map their environments then estimate their location within that environment in order to move. Robot vacuums rely on simultaneous localisation and mapping

(SLAM) algorithms, which innovatively have been crossed with the quantum qubit.

A University of Sydney team created an "adaptive algorithm that measures the performance of one qubit and uses that information to estimate the capabilities of nearby qubits…called Noise Mapping for Quantum Architectures. Instead of considering the singular environment of one qubit, the team automated and sped up the process by reducing the number of measurements and qubits required making quantum computing more effective than traditional robot-inspired techniques.

Legal Industry

The traditionally staid legal world, and its decision-making process is changing too. Some of the inherent benefits of leveraging machine learning in the legal field today include elimination or reduction of bias, data validation, precedent showcasing, the ability to identify corruption (via high human variance in decisions) and faster decision process (when judges leverage these tools). Areas of the legal field that already embrace AI include contract management and document review (incredibly fast comparison capability across hundreds of thousands of pages), client due diligence, and outcome prediction (incorporating factors such as the probability of winning or losing a case based on precedent, judge decision history and the current case). Market solutions include Ross Intelligence, eBrevia, ThoughtRiver, and LawGeex.

By integrating quantum computing not only are vastly greater stores of data more digestible, at an accelerated pace in many cases over classical computing and AI, but quantum offers a greater probability of accuracy. According to Steven De Schrijver in Who'sWhoLegal, "Some argue that quantum technology will be capable to predict the outcome of court cases… Some expect that quantum computers will perform complex tasks on a large scale with an efficiency and speed that surpasses human intelligence, including that of the best lawyers." The future has yet to be written, but advanced tech is well on the way to altering the foundations of the law.

Regulation, Errors & Decision-Making

In 2016, the General Data Protection Regulation went into effect in Europe with a view to protecting the consumer and their data. As more decisions by organizations are automated, legislators worry that automation will become the sole basis for decisions. With the advent of quantum computing that likelihood could increase as the efficiency and efficacy of automated decision-making improves. It remains to be seen how both manufacturers and buyers of quantum tech stacks comply with the regulations such as GDPR going forward.

In 2018, John Preskill, American theoretical physicist and the Richard P. Feynman Professor of Theoretical Physics at the California Institute of Technology, cautioned the world in the journal 'Quantum' about the impact of NISQ (or Noisy Intermediate-Scale Quantum) computers given their fidelity challenges due to noise and error correction. "Quantum computers with 50–100 qubits may be able to perform tasks which surpass the capabilities of today's classical digital computers, but noise in quantum gates will limit the size of quantum circuits that can be executed reliably…Quantum technologists should continue to strive for more accurate quantum gates and, eventually, fully fault-tolerant quantum computing." Significant breakthroughs have occurred since Preskill's caution, yet organizations would be wise to understand the true fidelity of systems being promoted to them for decision-making purposes.

Conclusion

Quantum computers bearing on how organizations make decisions in the future is expected to become heavily weighted in the effort to make faster, more accurate, lower energy, better long-term decisions. Whether in financial trade, autonomous vehicles, the legal field or others, quantum industry players will need to weigh the investments against the risks and regulations — yet another decision they have to make.

Chapter 12

Pharma & Biotech Research

On pure speculation, just an educated guess, I'd say that man is alive."
– Dr. Leonard McCoy to Spock, Star Trek

I have been writing for years about drug discovery and the implications of artificial intelligence on the pace and accuracy of drug research and development. Adding quantum computing to the mix is expected to advance drug design (as it did in the 2020 Covid-19 environment) and lead to personalized, customized prescription drugs for individuals. Companies like BASF, Biogen, Dow Chemical, Dupont and Amgen use quantum computing for catalyst and enzyme design, pharmaceuticals R&D, bioinformatics, and patient diagnosis.

When 2020 began, few would have believed the global changes that have occurred due to a microscopic virus, Covid-19. Worldwide shutdowns have been commonplace, the ubiquitous use of face masks, and predictions of case numbers continuing to grow. What, in this new reality does this have to do with a nascent technology like quantum computing? A great deal it appears.

Researching any new strain of virus can take years using traditional methods, including classical computing, on binary machines. In April of 2020, Canadian company ***D-Wave*** offered its quantum computing capabilities for free to Covid-19 researchers. The exciting part of this offer? Exponentially faster speeds in processing data and thus the analysis being conducted by virus researchers. It is not only to understand the virus and its mutations better but also to begin the development of vaccines to combat the pandemic.

While the coronavirus has reportedly caused over 3,000,000 deaths (at the time of writing according to the World Health Organization) globally, infectious diseases are responsible for over 13 million global deaths annually, according to the University of Virginia. According to the Association of the British Pharmaceutical Industry (ABPI), the historical average timeframe for pharmaceutical product development from drug discovery to licensing approval is 12.5 years. During that time, 5-10,000 drug candidates are whittled down to 10-20 likeliest solutions after 4.5 years, then down to 5-10 after another 2.5 years and down to 1-2 candidates within 11 years with another eight months to receive licensing approval. These are historical averages.

Understanding the impact or implications of such factors as urbanization, lab research, interaction patterns, anti-microbial resistance, ecological changes, population health, and more is challenging. Data science attempts to incorporate micro and macro complexities into traditional computation techniques to progress our understanding of the field of epidemiology. Simulating pandemics and epidemics virtually using AI, machine learning, and today's supercomputers consume vast amounts of processing power, with slower than desired results. Challenges for traditional computing capabilities arise as groups push the limits of scale and complexity in problems relating to the field of biology.

Predictions for Pharma and Quantum

Applications in healthcare on the horizon for quantum computing include drug discovery, clinical and care delivery, operations and supply chain management, cancer radiation therapy, pandemic management, genomics, protein structure predictions, anti-microbial resistance, surgical incisions, neuroscience and brain interfaces, clinical trial size and patient selection optimization and many more.

McKinsey suggests clinical trial planning optimization is a 2020 use case in pharma, while protein folding is a couple of years away, design of new molecules and chemicals a couple of years beyond that, virtual screening of drug candidates by 2026 and finally personalized medicine and drug recommendations by 2030.

Epidemiology

In a July 2020 article titled "Quantum Computing and Epidemiology: Research in the Time of CoViD-19", my co-author Mahmood Qasmi, founder of Transiotek, and I included elements of his April 2020 article titled "CoViD-19 Root-Cause Analysis and Monitoring Framework in the Wake of Varied Symptoms". The latter outlined how CoViD-19 is a manifestation of multiple independent physiological processes in the human body in response to the virus. Since antigen and antibody tests for CoViD-19 are still not on par with the needs of rapid diagnosis, he proposed a method for extensive remote monitoring to collect and analyze data on heart rate and blood pressure, as well as blood oxygenation. As such, large portions of a vulnerable population could benefit from this preliminary testing regimen, where interventional actions are taken for an individual only if monitored data indicates a progressively worsening condition. He also indicated how such monitoring data could provide a framework for advancing our knowledge of the progression and severity behaviours of this and similar contagious diseases in a population.

Being able to aggregate vast amounts of data, whether at a population level, or individual patient level through in-presence testing or smart device tracking, is essential to an improved understanding of the coronavirus and its symptoms, and effects. Taking on the challenge of how quantum computing can support the analysis of such data pools, in a shorter period of time is critical for the healthcare and pharma industries.

How Quantum Computing can help disease control?

Epidemics don't just erupt out of nothing: Imminent disease outbreaks can be modeled, and can help epidemiologists in disease control. While a lot of modeling effort goes into asking the right questions, optimizing the computing power to get meaningful results is still not possible without gross simplifications. For example, the traditional Susceptible-Infective-Removed (SIR) disease proliferation model embodies Non-deterministic Polynomial complexity in computing time. This means that while we are only able verify one pre-existing solution to this model at a time (remember, it is non-deterministic to begin with) we cannot even do so without incurring significant computational costs. In fact, model parameters can be so confounded sometimes, that even modern supercomputers cannot keep up with processing requirements. Some epidemiologists try to simplify these models by assuming all infectious individuals become removed (or re-susceptible) with a constant probability per unit time. But this does not adequately reflect ground truth, and can end up in grossly incorrect predictions.

Quantum computers can rise to the occasion to give researchers the much-needed computing boost in simulating SIR models for instance. Earlier this year, research from the University of Alabama demonstrated how compartmental models (used in SIR studies) could be implemented on quantum computers. If brought to market, such quantum computing infrastructure could help predict epidemics and global pandemics at a fraction of the time it takes on classical computers. Perhaps such studies could help prevent future waves of CoViD-19, or similar deadly disease outbreaks even before they happen.

How AI & QC are changing/will change the face of Epidemiology?

Another problem that epidemiologists aim to investigate is the optimal distribution of a vaccine or medication. The aim here is to determine the best possible way to distribute medication (answering the "where" and "when") to thwart the spread of disease in vulnerable populations. Imagine attempting to model such a scenario on a classical computer, and account for all possible variables including population size, cultural norms, living conditions, genetics and weather patterns, among a multitude of other parameters. In its simplest form, such combinatorial optimization would not be unlike the classic Traveling Salesperson Problem (TSP). Although TSP aims to determine the shortest possible route for a salesman to go through a city or between cities while visiting all potential clients, its computational complexity increases exponentially with each new client destination.

Machine learning and AI have shown great promise in providing optimal solutions for such problems. However, the multidimensional nature of TSP modeling stops classical computers dead in its tracks. For example, solving for the optimal route of a salesperson visiting 33,000 simulated destinations could take more than 15 years on a modern classical computer.

Interestingly, quantum computing is ideally suited to tackle such problems. Foremost example of this is a small scale near-real-time TSP solution obtained using D-Wave's quantum computer. If fully implemented, such computers could help in the fight against future epidemics to provide optimal solutions to vaccine and medication distribution models in real-time. That would certainly enable rapid mobilization of mass treatment regimen to help healthcare providers halt the spread of infectious diseases - not unlike how wild fires are put out today.

The global challenges of pandemics and epidemics are unlikely to vanish in the future of humanity, but the way in which we battle those eventualities will change and quantum computing will be one of our weapons in the attempt to defeat dangerous viruses.

While listening in on Canada's ground-breaking Digital Health & Discovery Platform (DHDP) a collaboration of 90 partners including the Federal Government to apply big data and AI to healthcare, I was astounded by the audacity of the venture. The DHDP is astounding in its breadth and scope of health-based and AI organizations coming together to develop a federated data platform where sensitive patient data goes unshared and there's a priority emphasis on privacy amongst partners.

It's certainly acknowledged by many that quantum computing is a relatively new technology, and in many cases been referred to as immature given the amount of 'noise', error reduction requirements, lack of available talent, lack of standardization, hardware costs and availability. Like Artificial Intelligence of a few years ago, concern around hype and inaccuracies remain factors in pursuing the technology as a viable solution. Yet every day breakthroughs are occurring and noise and errors are being reduced. Qubits (the quantum equivalent of digital bits) capacity is increasing, as are the number of applications/use cases, communities and hardware advances as we've discussed in this book. Large organizations are including quantum computing as part of their long-term strategy, but also with a fast-maturing ecosystem, considering more immediate applications.

D-Wave Systems Inc., a quantum computer manufacturer based in Burnaby, BC, is a world-renown for its optimization prowess leveraging quantum annealing (one of several approaches to quantum computing). D-Wave currently claims over 250 "user-developed early quantum applications... including airline scheduling, election modelling, quantum chemistry simulation..." Well, you get the idea. They have to date addressed a number of biological optimization problems including projects such as "Unconventional machine learning of genome-wide human cancer data" and "Quantum Annealing Approach to Molecule Unfolding".

Benefits for Researchers & Clinicians

Quantum computing has a vital role in research and drug development, both present and future. Practitioners in the healthcare research space are highly ensconced in patents and defensive publishing. Quantum computing as a tool in the hands of researchers can provide significant insights into complex pharmacological and biotech questions not available to today's classical computers or even supercomputers. Such a tool can accelerate the journey from concept to credibility.

Being able to aggregate vast amounts of data, whether at a population level, or individual patient level through in-presence testing or smart device tracking, is essential to an improved understanding of diseases and their symptoms and effects. According to Jessica Kent's Big Data to See Explosive Growth, Challenging Healthcare Organizations" which appeared in Health IT Analytics in 2018, suggested healthcare data was growing by 36% annually. The challenge is having so-called clean data AI and quantum algorithms can leverage. Efforts like DHDP provide hope for solving this challenge.

As Dawn Bell, Global Development Head of Novartis stated at the opening of the DHDP Session on February 24th, 2021 "Drug development is mainly an optimization problem… We need to be better at predicting toxicity and efficacy in humans…" going on to reaffirm the importance of understanding how solutions are predicted to bind to proteins.

Centric Consulting, a business and technology consulting firm headquartered in Dayton Ohio, suggests "Quantum's ability to compute at scale will allow clinicians to incorporate a vast number of cross-functional data sets into their patient risk factor models. For instance, we'll be able to analyze environmental databases to evaluate the effect of pollution on a patient's health history." Centric goes on to suggest leveraging QC for processing imagery at scale, implementing precision medicine recognizing the individual physiology of patients, and selecting patients for clinical trials more accurately.

Further, consider the 2020 report from IBM Institute for Business Value titled "Exploring quantum computing use cases for healthcare: Accelerate diagnoses, personalize medicine, and optimize pricing". The report argues "As access to health-relevant data sources continues to grow, the potential for the combination of quantum computing and classical modeling to save lives and reduce costs increases."

Imagine adding the DHDP data pool to AI, classical modelling and quantum computing to three key focus areas namely: "Diagnostic assistance: i.e. medical imaging, cell classification, biomarkers and 'omics"; Precision medicine: personalized customized interventions/treatments; Pricing: improve risk analysis and pricing computations."

A resounding celebration of the Canadian spirit to come together to share data in a secure manner through DHDP. By partnering across organizations, combining AI including machine learning with problems in healthcare, DHDP plans to address the age-old data challenges every organization faces and providing a go-forward path. Combining the DHDP approach with quantum computing should offer up a strong dose of hope for global citizens.

Chapter 13
Security & Cryptography

"Digital is the main reason just over half the companies on the Fortune 500 have disappeared since the year 2000"

– Pierre Nanterne, CEO of Accenture

Speaking at the Vancouver International Privacy & Security Summit this year about quantum cryptography and post-quantum cryptography reaffirmed my belief in how important the technology would become in the future to address some incredibly important and complex security demands worldwide. My host and primary sponsor of the Summit, the British Columbia Institute of Technology, is a leading voice in this challenging world. The Summit addressed the key security issues of the day being fought through government and private initiatives and investments. As we progress as a digital society, privacy and security demands continue to grow.

The challenge with breaking encryption codes today is the incredibly large numbers involved and a brute force approach requiring large amounts of time. The RSA (Rivest–Shamir–Adleman) public-key cryptosystem is one of the oldest used for secure data transmission. With the advent of quantum computing, isolating these numbers could occur in just seconds or moments, rendering RSA obsolete. According to Dustin Moody, a mathematician at NIST, the US National Institute of Standards and Technology "Researchers have known for decades that if a large-scale quantum computer could be built, it could do some pretty big calculations that would threaten the cryptosystems that we rely on today for security."

In a typical description of a quantum message, we have two players, Alice and Bob (A & B). Alice wants to send a message to Bob. Along with the message is a secret key. To secure the message it and the key are scrambled in transmission, then decrypted by Bob on the other end using his secret key. The challenge comes when someone (say Carol or C) tries to intercept the message to steal or copy it. Both Alice and Bob want secure methods to communicate. So does the rest of the world.

What is a public key cryptosystem (PKC)? While RSA is not the only one, it is the most well-known since its inception in 1977. In a PKC, the public component is the encryption key (EK), while the private component is the decryption key. The EK is created by the user based on two large prime numbers and a separate value. Such messages can only be decoded by a person who has the prime numbers which are factored (which is extremely difficult to do) and no published methods exist demonstrating the ability to defeat it if a large enough key is applied. Because RSA's algorithm is considered slow, shared keys are transmitted with RSA and then bulk encryption-decryption occurs.

The quantum algorithm considered likely to break RSA and classical computing cryptography is Shor's Algorithm. Originated by Peter Shor of MIT in 1994, the algorithm factors values, and while most quantum computers do not have enough qubits to break the encryption, many feel it's just a matter of time (and enough qubits). Yet such an algorithm alone may not be enough to guarantee secure communications.

According to Dr. Mattia Fiorentini, Head of Artificial Intelligence of Cambridge Quantum Computing in the UK, "Quantum systems, and qubits can generate streams of random bits that are certified to be random. This can be readily used in current encryption protocols to generate more resistant cryptographic keys.... Fortunately, cracking cryptography with quantum computers is a task that will be out of reach of available quantum hardware for at least a decade or more." So quantum computers being able to crack classical computer encryption is a viable eventuality but not yet.

Canada & Cybersecurity

$80 million invested in a cybersecurity network by the Canadian government, as part of the country's Digital Charter, is a significant signal of support for R&D, commercialization, talent, and collaboration of academia and industry. Funded over four years starting in 2021, the program is pan-Canadian, and addresses concerns from individuals and businesses about their trust in data privacy, security and competitiveness as the population goes increasingly digital as are all countries.

Cybersecurity as an industry in Canada is not minor. In fact, GDP increased by over $2 billion, and added over 22,000 jobs in 2018 alone. Spending by businesses in Canada exceeded $7 billion for prevention detection and recovery from cybersecurity incidents. The federal government recognizes and is addressing cybersecurity challenges through investments like this one. It will be interesting to see what role quantum cryptography plays within the Canadian security ecosystem.

NIST Quantum Cryptography Competition

After spending more than three years examining new approaches to encryption and data protection that could defeat an assault from a quantum computer, the National Institute of Standards and Technology (NIST) has winnowed the 69 submissions it initially received down to a final group of 15. NIST has now begun the third round of public review. This "selection round" will help the agency decide on the small subset of these algorithms that will form the core of the first post-quantum cryptography standard. The winner is expected to be selected in 2022.

NIST's third phase of the Post-Quantum Cryptography Standardization Process with seven third round finalists and eight alternate candidates under consideration will be presented at the next NIST PQC Standardization Conference, to be held in June 2021. "At the end of this round, we will choose some algorithms and standardize them," said NIST mathematician Dustin Moody. "We intend to give people tools that are capable of protecting sensitive information for the foreseeable future, including after the advent of powerful quantum computers.

One approach, which includes the majority of finalists incorporates huge grids of billions of points over thousands of dimensions requiring the decrypter to navigate one point to another. This approach is called lattice-based cryptography. The National Security Agency (NSA) in the United States stated their confidence in the lattice approach yet there are some challenges in terms of the size of the cryptography and widespread scalability. Yet given the technology is changing so rapidly, a new solution may emerge as late as 2022 as the competition is being decided.

Quantum Key Distribution

Fear not totally for data security however, as a new development called quantum key distribution has arrived with the ability to encrypt communications using entangled qubit keys. While some argue QKD is not the solution, others suggest QKD is viable. Why? QKD systems authenticate at both ends of the exchange, securing the communication seamlessly according to John Prisco, Security CEO and Founder of Safe Quantum Inc. When someone, not the intended receiver, tries to decrypt the message, it is immediately destroyed. So, eavesdropping on communications over a quantum internet should be impossible. Data could not be stolen or copied, and originators would know, in real time, if someone intercepted a message. New QKD systems operate in such a way that keys are redirected rapidly and randomly making user performance impact essentially invisible, and the interloper will be shut out.

One challenge is that the quantum internet which will be based on photons or light-based communication will likely be transported over optical fibers already in place, so the implementation of the quantum internet could emerge more quickly than a quantum encryption/ decryption standard. According to Peter Limacher, quantum expert at SAP Security Research, "Organizations need to move ahead in parallel with quantum hardware development so software applications are ready when quantum communication networks go live." In-ground fiber is suitable to support QKD and the technology is being developed to minimize distance limitations between endpoints.

Limacher attended the Quantum Internet Alliance (part of the European Union's Horizon 2020 research and innovation program) hackathon in 2019 where academics and industry players explored improving the Open Secure Sockets Layer (SSL) library, the vehicle to implement internet security protocols. The hackathon derived three major protocols aligning with business communication trust priority use cases namely QKD, quantum digital signature, and quantum money.

ID Quantique Example

Consider the work of ID Quantique (IDQ), a Swiss-based multinational company which bills itself as "the world leader in Quantum-Safe Security & Quantum Sensing". IDQ, maker of the Quantis Quantum Random Number Generator chip is an EU Open QKD standards contributor, which works with clients such as Standard Chartered and SAE. IDQ states its QKD ensures a "provably secure key exchange, alerting any potential eavesdropping, as well as providing forward secrecy of the encryption keys."

IDQ's chip in mobile phones (like the Samsung Galaxy smartphone) enriches application security for payment services, identification services and cryptocurrencies. Their signal app helps identify whether you are communicating securely. In banking, their Digital Trust Platform operates in support of central bank currency. The IDQ Cerberis 3 hardware supports secure utility company operations. Their solutions integrate with different network encryption solutions.

In 2021, there already are quantum key distribution solutions for securing your organization, pursuing data integrity, and demonstrating to stakeholders your organizations cybersecurity commitment. IBM, another leader in the quantum security space launched Quantum Safe Cryptography for Key Management and Application Transactions. IBM is combining its quantum computing hardware leadership and open Qiskit programming with encryption and data security to promote the safe evolution of quantum computing. The company states it is rotecting data within applications (ie encryption within databases), and IBM offers Extended IBM Cloud Hyper Protect Crypto Service, encryption schemes in databases and digital signature validation. Other security related services include IBM Cloud Data Shield, research and IBM Cloud Security and Compliance Center.

Some like Gilles Brassard, Professor at the University of Montreal and co-inventor along with Charlie Bennett of IBM of what we today call quantum cryptography, argue that China is ahead of the rest of the world in the field with a 2,000-kilometre optical fibre network of trusted relays with quantum key distribution between Beijing and Shanghai completed in 2017. The quantum security race is in full flight.

Post-Quantum Cryptography

If security is your area of interest you may have heard the term post-quantum cryptography. So what exactly is the difference between quantum cryptography and post-quantum cryptography (PQC)? We've discussed the idea that quantum cryptography will 1) provide a higher level of security and 2) be able to break traditional encryption. It's natural for organizational to ask the next level questions – will my quantum systems be safe from other quantum computers? PQC refers to cryptographic algorithms considered secure against attacks by other quantum computers, making these systems virtually unhackable.

Conclusion

As a business leader, one of your top organizational priorities is data security and privacy, whether yours or your customers. So being confident in a new vehicle such as the second or quantum internet will be paramount. Exchanging encryption keys between data centers internally or externally over optical wire will require quantum key distribution. Even if someone were to intercept data, they may experience multiple key encryptions to solve. If you are leading an organization, you should be considering IDQ's Five Key takeaways for organizations: 1) Do not delay 2) Know Your Data 3) Improve Key Generation 4) Pursue Crypto-Agility and 5) One size does not fit all.

Given the pace of change in the quantum world in terms of technologies, standards, benefits and risks, it is crucial for organizations to immediately start to understand the dynamics of quantum security and cryptography.

Chapter 14
Finance

"JPMorgan Chase wants to be ready for the quantum leap"
Company website

Business leaders are concerned about food products from field to fork, chemical evolution from concept to customer, and investment products from portfolio picking to performance. Today, all are beginning to leverage quantum computing.

Goldman Sachs recently predicted that commercially viable quantum computing would be available within five years – ahead of what many believe is a reasonable time frame. Moving forecasts and goalposts forward for the financial services industry (in this case pricing complex derivatives) may not be surprising for some considering advances being made in the quantum computing field. While the forecast doesn't predict universal fault tolerant computers, for business the goal is support through reliable quantum technology in achieving KPI's.

In the field of investment portfolio management, the task seems rather simple on the surface: achieving maximum reward with lowest possible risk. Yet managing a diverse portfolio of financial assets is a challenging and complex balancing act. Simply trying to assess the "number of possible configurations for a portfolio of eight assets in which transactions are performed every month for four years is greater than the number of atoms in the known universe" according to one quantum vendor.

Yet that's the environment in which quantum computers should thrive. Uncertainty, complexity, massive data pools, market volatility, derivatives, transaction costs, regulations, exchange traded funds or ETF's and numerous other diverse input factors, and a variety of risk/return calculations are just some of the components of selecting investment portfolios. Computational limits of classical computers, even those powered by artificial intelligence algorithms are challenged to optimize portfolios, and scenario development.

Should your organization be one of the first to accurately and reliably identify optimal investment portfolios, and light-speed methods to rebalance, surely you will leave the competition in the dust. Identifying unique arbitrage opportunities, satisfying dynamic compliance requirements, faster market reactions and more accurate market predictions are being promoted under the quantum computing umbrella. However, caution must reign. The promise is endless though merely an opening salvo. Quantum computing is still an immature technology, and despite recent breakthroughs and progressive use cases, some experts, as we've discussed, continue to suggest its reliable future is five or even 10 years away.

Returning to Goldman Sachs, their efforts with QCWare (a company populated by quantum algorithm experts) suggest that a less than perfect quantum computer could still hold a 10-fold improvement in Monte Carlo simulations within five years, rather than waiting for the perfect quantum (fault tolerant) technology. The search for quantum advantage over classical computers continues today apace as businesses look to immediately gain from investments in quantum solutions. Problems that defy classical computers (where quantum supremacy would reign) do exist yet that is not where business leaders are necessarily looking today. Shareholders demand reasonable returns while investor analysts, venture capital firms and others with a primarily financial focus expect business leaders and their organizations to produce. Waiting for the perfect quantum computer is not their priority.

Goldman Sachs' head of research, Paul Burchard, argues that pricing derivatives demands a "very large computing bill we pay each year…". Real-time response to clients over the phone would be a vastly improved service over today's need to wait hours to quote prices as the bank runs its calculations. Quantum-powered Monte Carlo simulations calculating future probabilities would generate faster responses. Even if the optimal quantum solution does not present itself immediately, (and one merely arrives at the same answer but in faster time), Goldman Sachs and QCWare are pursuing a better-than-today solution which is less exhaustive, and less prone to errors creeping in from qubit decoherence.

Portfolio Optimization

To drill down on portfolio optimization, let's look at two recent examples. In the first, Canadian quantum computer manufacturer D-Wave partnered with KPMG and a team of researchers from the Technical University of Denmark (DTU) to run a portfolio optimization model on D-Wave's 2,000-qubit quantum annealing processor.

The pilot project "to determine which stocks to buy and sell for maximum return" compares results to classical computing. Their conclusion? D-Wave quantum annealing hardware "performed better and faster than other methods, while being capable of resolving larger problems". The study concluded however the technology illustrated ease of programming and scalability issues.

The risk return model selected for this exercise was the Markowitz model which chooses securities that do not 'move' exactly together, illustrating to investors ways to reduce their risk, while allocating a fixed budget to a grouping of assets to maximize returns. The traditional challenge in portfolio optimization is the number of variables inherent in the risk/return calculation, which for classical computers, even those infused with artificial intelligence or classified as supercomputers, are challenged to solve. Increase the number of assets, the difficulty level rises. Incorporate more risk factors like the economy, leadership, industry change, technology evolution…the list goes on and so does the complexity. Which is where quantum computing comes in. The world's largest banks like JP Morgan Chase are investing research teams and funds to solve complex portfolio optimization problems in mere minutes.

So how is this accomplished? Certainly the largest banks have multiple hardware and vendor options to select from whether they be superconducting (IBM, Google), ion trap (Honeywell, IonQ), photonic (Xanadu) or quantum annealing as offered by D-Wave. For this project, KPMG et al selected D-Wave due to its optimization experience.

In the case of quantum annealing, researchers must formulate the equation into a model called a quadratic unconstrained binary optimization (QUBO) problem. Unlike other systems that are gate-based, annealing technology manipulates the environment around the system permitting the device to determine a ground state or in this case the optimized portfolio. Unlike other systems, annealing means D-Wave can leverage more qubits than other devices, which count is 5,000 on the latest Advantage/Leap devices.

Setting up the trial, the team decided to run the problem for 65 assets. They elected to benchmark the processor performance against a brute force solution which had an upper limit of 25 assets, confirmed equal reliability, then proved that as they added assets, the quantum processor "overtook brute force as the fastest method. "Despite the obvious advantage, research team members cautioned any exuberance for more study and comparisons against supercomputer capabilities which is likely prudent. "As the portfolio size was increased, a degradation in the quality of the solutions found by quantum annealing was indeed observed," says a leading team member. "But after optimization, the solutions were still competitive and were more often than not able to beat simulated annealing." While we may not yet be at the portfolio optimization plug and play level, the future is promising.

Risk/Return ratio measures

Consider that in the investing world today there are multiple risk/return measures. Beyond the Markowitz model, there are numerous others. The Capital Asset Pricing Model or CAPM describes the relationship between systematic risk and expected return or assets, particularly stocks and includes the risk-free rate, the beta of the investment and the market risk premium. Modigliani squared (M2) measures the "returns of the portfolio, adjusted for the risk of the portfolio relative to that of some benchmark (e.g., the market)". It arguably has an advantage over the Sharpe ratio as M2 is in units of percent return making it more intuitive to interpret. The Sortino ratio measures the risk-adjusted return of an investment asset, portfolio, or strategy. But unlike the Sharpe ratio, it only penalizes returns falling below "a user-specified target or required rate of return, while the Sharpe ratio penalizes both upside and downside volatility equally." The Monte Carlo model is used to "predict the probability of different outcomes when the intervention of random variables is present. Monte Carlo simulations help to explain the impact of risk and uncertainty in prediction and forecasting models." Each model provides a slightly different outcome based on the duration of the data period under study (which should also include several business cycles), additional factors like dividend history, and should be compared against each other for validation purposes.

Canadian bank, The Bank of Nova Scotia (or Scotiabank) is collaborating with The Bank of Montreal (or BMO) and Xanadu (the Toronto-based photonic quantum computing specialist) to investigate accelerating the speed and accuracy of computations in trading. The POC leveraged a Xanadu quantum Monte Carlo algorithm to simulate it on various trading products resulting in what Scotiabank programmer Tom Pickering called "… a thousand-fold-plus speed increase on the most complicated calculations we do. And speed over repeated calculations gives us better accuracy."

Another example is also based on the D-Wave quantum annealing computer this time with Multiverse Computing, BBVA and Bankia (MBB). Unlike the KPMG effort, the Multiverse group focused on the Sharpe Ratio and Modern Portfolio theory. The Sharpe Ratio for example is a measurement of the performance of an investment as compared to a risk-free asset, after adjusting for its risk) The ratio suggests total portfolio risk should be represented by the standard deviation of returns (and a normal distribution) despite the market not necessarily having such a distribution.. The project is also based on Modern Portfolio Theory, based on Markowitz's work, which states that risk-averse investors can construct portfolios to maximize expected return based on a given level of market risk, although it does not consider downside risk (small declines or spectacular falls). More post-modern portfolio theory takes both into account.

Certainly financial giants like JP Morgan Chase, Goldman Sachs, and BBVA have invested heavily early on in this new technology's maturity as have global energy, pharmaceuticals and telecom/media firms. Lagging far behind in terms of existing use cases, according to the 2020 McKinsey report, are travel, consumer goods and insurance.

Insurance

What about the insurance industry? Insurers attempt to maximize premium revenues while minimizing risks. Fraught with such risks, dependent upon analysts taking into account as many factors as is feasible to assess the exposure an insurer is taking on by providing insurance to clients in the case of fire, flood, directors and officers, and a myriad of other types.

Yet what if insurers could accurately simulate weather patterns, enhance predictive capabilities for catastrophes or driving patterns. A quantum computing tool could augment the value of the insurers' underwriting function.

Quantum computing is a rising phenomenon in the Gartner Hype Cycle. The hype cycle, the graphical representation of technologies' maturity, adoption & applications across industries, and the benefits they bring to the businesses. Quantum computing is expected to become one of the greatest disruptions of the age as it can process huge datasets in a fraction of a second that would have previously taken days and weeks. It can also calculate almost any kind of risks, such as the impact of an approaching hurricane. Only the constraint of access to data might limit improved risk assessment in future.

According to the Finadium Editorial Team "Quantum computing's ability to accurately simulate risk scenarios, optimize portfolios and quickly sift through large unstructured datasets to train ML algorithms for fraud detection and enhanced customer targeting, can deliver significant benefits to the financial services industry." Mitch Wein and Tom Kramer offer various use cases of quantum computing in "Quantum Computing and Insurance: Overview and Potential Players." However, this technology isn't yet available for commercial use, unlike AI. The insurance industry is simplifying many of its back and front-office operations through AI, it is still restricted by barriers of binary computing. Quantum computing can unlock and change the entire dynamics of how insurance companies carry out complex calculations.

Insurtech companies are creating and testing solutions around this approach and its effects will soon be visible. Consider the case of Willis Towers Watson. CEO John Haley recently stated, "Willis Towers Watson provides advanced analytics tools to over 1,000 insurers around the world, allowing them to quantify risk and allocate capital efficiently. Current modelling techniques to quantify risk require a huge amount of computing power, using thousands of computers over many hours. The better the models, the more efficiently our clients can use their capital to manage risk. Quantum computing offers us the chance to look at our clients' problems in a different way. By focusing on how we would model the problems on quantum computers when they become available at scale, we are able to redefine the problems and speed up our solutions on existing hardware today."

Insurance firms should look to their industry associations, quantum meetups and the February 2021 publication by Anahita Zardoshti for Lloyds titled "The impacts of quantum computing on insurance" for a complete review of the state of the industry relative to this new technology.

Chapter 15

Manufacturing & Power

Today's manufacturing sector faces a myriad of challenges including tariffs, foreign dumping, skilled labour shortages, cost escalations and more. So, executives are looking for ways to automate repetitive tasks and transition employees on to more value-add activities. In a 2020 Deloitte Insights study, they argued that "manufacturing leaders will likely need to understand the following to differentiate themselves… The pace of disruption that digitization brings, and the investments manufacturers can make to best position themselves to succeed." In the same study, Deloitte argues that while manufacturers will be heavily disrupted by digitization, many are not prepared for the transition. So, we would argue the time to plan is now.

People use tools to solve problems and quantum computing is merely another tool. An incredibly fast processing tool. One that will change the face of so many industries in the future, much like artificial intelligence is doing today.

If you're in manufacturing, quantum computing is for you. Problems involving supply chain optimization are many and varied including distribution, production and procurement. As QC evolves, companies will leverage the new technology to identify multiple truck load scenarios, store floor configurations, digital twinning of assets, and eventually the end-to-end supply chain. Companies like Airbus, Lockheed Martin, Honeywell, BMW, Raytheon and Bosch can use quantum computing for chip layout optimization, fault analysis, and material science to name a few.

Computational Fluid Dynamics

In this section, we take on the challenge of a key manufacturing industry research tool, namely computation fluid dynamics or CFD. CFD is used for product development and fluid flow problems, providing solutions for optimizing manufacturing equipment and processes. It is also used for specialized, high-value problems to understand fluid behaviour for certain given conditions.

According to Marcin Rojek, co-founder of byteLAKE, Computational Fluid Dynamics tools combine numerical analysis and algorithms to solve fluid flow problems. They are used to model fluid density, velocity, pressure, temperature, and chemical concentrations in relation to time and space. A range of industries such as automotive, chemical, aerospace, biomedical, power and energy, and construction rely on fast CFD analysis turnaround time. It is a key part of their design workflow to understand and design how liquids and gases flow and interact with surfaces. Typical applications include weather simulations, aerodynamic characteristics modeling and optimization, and petroleum mass flow rate assessment.

A lot of CFD modeling effort goes into asking the right questions and optimizing the computing power to get meaningful results – including mesh size, geometry, and fluid characteristics. These simulations currently take up to a month to run with one set of parameters because of the complexity. Parameters often include fluids, density, velocity, elements, purity, equipment specifics, air mixing, and more.

How AI & QC are changing/will change the face of CFD

Most of the leading insights about quantum computing originate from academic and research environments. Take for example, MIT, my alma mater. Professor Seth Lloyd and team experienced a breakthrough recently applying algebraic equations (used also in solving CFD problems) to bridge the gap between CFD and quantum computing algorithms.

In 2018, Steijl and Barakos published a paper called "Parallel evaluation of quantum algorithms for computational fluid dynamics". Sounds complex right? Well, while it was complex, what this pair tried to do was better understand the noise and error impact within quantum computer algorithms (as they were in 2018) within a flow solution. They found that "meaningful flow simulations can be performed using a hybrid classical/quantum hardware approach."

So, work is being done specific to CFD and QC, but what are the benefits and what are the realities?

Increased Number of Viable Designs

Growing the capability within an organization to use CFD in conjunction with QC could have breakthrough benefits in the long term as a research department could make use of several thousand simulations to develop better manufactured parts (lighter, stronger, cheaper, more consistent, better quality) or to solve production problems that required deep study using CFD today. These solutions could be optimized over several thousand scenarios, using more parameters, if the computation time was reduced using QC.

Because of the computational power needed to run CFD simulations, assumptions are made about some model inputs. This would be less relevant when using QC because more models could be run. So, these inputs could be varied until the model is more accurate when compared to the real world. Then that model could be used to hone in on a better solution before starting trials in the plant.

Reduce Modelling Time

Solving computational fluid dynamics problems using traditional methods requires a lot of time and a lot of effort. For researchers who rely on data, and their interrelationships, running simulations to understand complex dependencies is an everyday task.

Combining AI, QML and quantum computing will offer faster computing (e.g. architectures that are optimized for high volume, rapid, physics-based calculations) and have multiple effects on CFD modeling and use for manufacturing. AI models have been developed to simulate the results of physics-based models with fair results, but a lot of training data is required to get AI models of comparable accuracy for a given problem. QC would not only allow for faster training of AI models, it could also allow for multiple variations of the research goal to be simulated and compared in seconds instead of days or weeks.

In one example, a CFD simulation exercise was performed by Germany's Renumic GmbH and UberCloud with the objective to decrease solving a fluid flow problem by 1000 times with the same accuracy as a traditional CFD solution process. The exercise found, not surprisingly with large amounts of data, they had better accuracy, six times faster than the traditional process, with tens of thousands of samples available in hours rather than days. Add the capabilities of quantum computing and that time span could eventually be minutes.

Realities of Investing in Quantum Computing

Four years ago, when artificial intelligence was still a nascent concept compared to where it is today, few people globally believed in its capabilities. Four years on, artificial intelligence is embedded in our smartphones, our online movie platforms, our research environments, even our car GPS'. I believe that quantum computing will have a similar trajectory. Yet I also acknowledge business leaders must consider the risks, compliance, rewards and cost considerations for QC & CFD going into the future.

At this point in time, investing in quantum computing is likely best entered into as a partnership between academic institutions, quantum computing firms like Honeywell, D-Wave and IBM, and with research arms of companies that already use CFD to good effectiveness. Having that expertise built into your company and/or your strategic partnerships will be key to leveraging QC in the future.

There are still concerns about the errors in QC computing and comparable results may be as much as 10 years off for some applications, but this is the time horizon of difficult research programs and considering QC as one arm to a comprehensive research program will mean early and quick adoption when technology is proven.

To minimize business risk and build capability, business leaders can start out with pilots and small use cases, like adopting any new digital tool. With low-risk investment in AI/QC at the small scale, leaders could demonstrate competency and build out capability prior to large scale investment. This will increase the trust in results when the time comes for those larger investments.

Quantum computing is considered by the financial services industry as an emerging technology with high potential business impact, second only to artificial intelligence. The manufacturing industry, and CFD participants more specifically, will benefit from advances in technology like quantum computing, however the time is now to start planning for the introduction of such capabilities within your own organization.

Power Generation

The power generation industry has its share of challenges from talent succession to regulation to cybersecurity to driving operational excellence. Despite the power of digitalization, these challenges can be barriers to the automation being achieved by other industries, yet pioneering industry players are overcoming these challenges. Energy companies like BP and Dubai Electricity and Water Company use quantum computing for network design, energy distribution and oil well optimization.

Operational excellence, which is a priority for these companies, includes a myriad of factors beyond simply supplying power such as making it affordable with high uptime, maintaining vast stores of equipment, not to mention public and environmental safety.

Physical resources dependent on technology for maintenance assessments will derive value from quantum computing in asset degradation modelling and optimization of utility systems. Moving from real-time data comparison to prescribed rules or models, to probabilistic evaluation for cost savings, and product or asset replacement on a system-wide basis becomes possible through quantum computing.

New dynamics in the power generation and energy grid ecosystem provide for the introduction of new ideas and computational tools. Increasing complexity in load balancing with increasing decentralization (greater distribution of energy resource and connected devices) of the power system and erratic consumption.

In this section, we break down three areas of the energy sectors primary applications, namely oversight and management of the grid infrastructure, the electrical system and the energy market, and the opportunities for quantum computing. Those involved with the grid infrastructure, for example, must focus on locating facilities, scheduling of maintenance and planning for renewable energy sources. Quantum computing is ideally suited to complex problems with numerous factors or inputs. In scheduling, power industry leaders must consider personnel, equipment availability, sensor monitors data, weather, financial resources, local government restrictions and more. In selecting energy facilities, managers consider operational costs, local zoning, sustainability issues, proximity, long term needs, community demands, all in the name of optimizing their facility choice. Balancing sustainability goals with commercial feasibility requires a host of factors to be considered, including the above to mix renewable sources of energy with more traditional methods in a hybrid offering.

The electrical system focuses on the monitoring of electrical flow, constant balancing of generation and consumption, while working with neighboring jurisdictions for the ingress and egress of their electricity generation and needs. Electrical systems evolve with new technologies resulting in improved network efficiencies and scheduling, and potentially reduced costs. Insights into such changes at an increasingly more detailed level through QC analysis and optimizing power flow continuously requires complex computations in real time. Finally, voltage controls and grid resilience through the optimization of how and where batteries, heat pumps, voltage regulators and capacitor banks are situated. In the market, storage of electricity needs to be optimized with planning for storage and reserves, unit commitment schedule effectiveness needs to be re-optimized and load management optimization in terms of pricing, generation and demand.

Microsoft is looking to redefine the power industry using quantum computing with goals of lowering emissions and creating more efficient electrical power systems. Researchers at Microsoft are beginning with quantum-inspired code run on conventional computers to perform grid optimization applications before scaling up on quantum hardware. The algorithm for unit commitment identifies the optimal resources to run given forecasted loads, generative efficiencies and capacities. The algorithm was proven to outperform classical solutions, even being run on conventional computers. Imagine the gain on quantum computers.

The Dubai Electricity and Water Authority is a leading light in the power generation ecosystem, leveraging its partnership with Microsoft and its Azure Quantum cloud environment to test its algorithms for real world data and solutions.

In terms of wind power, quantum computing is ideally suited to support the location of wind turbines, leveraging historical data from climate databases, geographic information systems and models. And where renewable energy is being fed back into the grid from smart cities and smart homes, quantum computing can support the optimization of reliable power sharing and generation in the largest grid systems. Hybrid systems (like solar and wind) have their own data sharing challenges and quantum could "track demand, predict peaks in consumption, coordinate energy storage, and manage resources could dramatically boost efficiency and so pave the way for cheaper, more reliable power." according to IEEE.

Chapter 16
Retail

"What scares me about this is that you know more about my customers after three months than I know after 30 years." Tesco Chairman, (1995) Lord MacLaurin discussing off-line customer data analytics

In 1995, Tesco, the UK groceries retailer, announced the introduction of loyalty cards for customers. What derived from this launch was much more than repeat purchases. The vast amount of data that could be churned through off-line data analytics drove a significantly better understanding of customer preferences and habits providing the opportunity for more personalized offers. Such a huge amount of customer demographic and preference data input into an optimized customer offering with high accuracy and real time speed remains beyond today's classical computing power. Thus, the importance of quantum computers in retail.

What demands exist in the retail environment that might necessitate a quantum computing solution? Here is a brief list:

- Perishable inventory within a complex and changing supply chain.
- Long lead times for some products
- Short shelf-life for some products including fresh foods
- Dynamic, real-time response
- Optimized customer experience
- Waste minimization
- Minimization of warehousing costs
- The preponderance of SKU's
- Demands for simple interfaces for users
- Accurate forecasting solutions without levering up headcount
- Balance high growth products supply
- Multiple store interaction in franchise environments

Marks and Spencer (M&S), another UK-based retail chain serves over 30 million customers from 1400+ stores and 35 websites. For a 137-year old company, marching into the 2020's has been challenging. The pandemic contributed to M&S' first loss in 94 years, along with layoffs and the closure of stores. M&S has over 6,400 core food catalogue products as well as special occasion foods to track and forecast. To that end M&S updated core systems starting in 2008 and engaged vendors with a quantum mindset to address many of the retail optimization issues above. "Quantum has played a key role in helping M&S getting the right products to our customers at a time when shoppers are offered and expect a rich array of choices," said Steve Rowe, as Executive Director, Food, Marks and Spencer's in 2015 about a key vendor. In 2018, M&S announced their intention to create a data skills academy for over 1,000 towards M&S becoming a more digital business. Now M&S Chief Executive Officer Steve Rowe said in the 2019 Corporate Report that "Over the past two years we have built a substantially new leadership team, bringing fresh perspective, energy and challenge to a business held back by deeply entrenched cultural norms." Retail is changing and so will its technology.

Today's pervasive customer demands for customized services (personalized recommendations for movies, videos, podcasts, clothing, etc.) has created a major challenge for traditional computing. Retailers need an IT strategy that envelopes their business as well as the external web.

In 2019, Fujitsu & teknowlogy published a report about retail and technology titled "Is Business Ready to Make the Quantum Leap?". They identified several findings from the 300 senior executives surveyed from enterprises in North America, the UK and Ireland, Germany, Spain and the Nordic region. At the time of the study in 2019, only 15% of retail companies surveyed were considering exploring quantum computing. Not even exploring yet.

It appeared that business leaders, particularly in retail organizations were not bought in to the concept of investing in quantum computing. Despite the majority (64%) believing that "being able to undertake faster, more effective product or service development would have huge potential benefits for key elements of their business or their entire organization" that did not necessarily mean quantum computers. So, was it a question of timing before the retail sector took notice since 79% believe that "Quantum Computing will transform their industry sector" and over half thought the transformation would affect their own business? A substantial 89% felt that existing computing power was holding back their ability to optimize calculations, yet they were not willing to wait for the advent and maturation of the "experimental" quantum computer (66%).

Yet not everyone is waiting. A grocery retailer in Western Canada, Save-On Foods, partnered recently with its local quantum computing partner D-Wave systems of Burnaby, BC to pilot grocery optimization reducing how long at least one important optimization task takes each week from 25 hours to just 2 minutes of calculations. Focusing on in-store logistics within one location, the reduction in computing time means reduced cost, faster decision-making, better store processing and the ability to redirect computing to other tasks. Running simulations with more variables has optimized Save-On Foods performance. Save-On Foods engineers reached out to D-Wave for this first instance and are looking to the partnership for other stores and other business challenges. D-Wave's 5,000 qubit quantum annealing processor successfully demonstrated its computing power to Save-On executives.

Quantum in retail is not restricted to groceries. A 10-year collaboration between IBM and the Cleveland Clinic promises to generate new discoveries in healthcare through the combination of QC, AI and cloud technologies. The clinic will be the world's first private company to house an IBM quantum computer on premises and plans to follow with a 1,000-qubit system in the future. Crunching mountains of data, which is a primary value-add of quantum computing, is the goal to support research into drug discovery, population health, genomics and more inside what is called the "The Discovery Accelerator". The Cleveland Clinic intends to remotely design and synthesize molecules, research viral and bacterial genomes through the more rapid analysis of structured and unstructured data.

Process optimization and research are not the only impacts quantum computing is having on retail. Gaining greater insights into unique customer preferences is every retailer's goal to strengthen their ties and create repeat business and customer loyalty. Quantum computing's ability to digest and large quantities of inputs like customer buying history, location, income levels, product trends, special offers etc. can enhance the competitiveness of retailer organizations providing convenient shopping experiences.

Collecting data from a myriad of sensors in warehouses, distribution centres, factories and on trucks provide greater transparency into retail goods flow, forecasting and operationalization. All creating vast amounts of data, for which optimization is a prime target. Robot and human path efficiency in warehouses, accelerating machine learning algorithms, optimizing sensor placement are all tasks ideally suited for quantum computing.

At NRF 2021, the large virtual retail conference held in January 2021, Fujitsu shared a presentation on how it was bringing quantum computing-inspired benefits and technology to address problems in retail that classical computers could not. The 'Digital Annealer' they introduced promised to offer real-time optimization at a scalable level.

New solutions for retail optimization are evolving for business leaders and the time is now to start understanding the opportunities and implications for the industry.

Chapter 17

Traffic & Roads Management

"The spread of intelligent transportation systems in urban cities has caused heavy computational loads, requiring a novel architecture for managing large-scale traffic."
— Daniel Inoue et al, Nature

More than 50% of the world's population is living in cities today, generating billions of data points daily. Future smart cities will be highly dependent on massive volumes of data – data that the internet of things autonomously collects and processes by artificial intelligence technologies employed today. Quantum computing can exponentially change the smart city's landscape by processing vast amounts of data that classical systems fail to understand and comprehend, leaving no stone unturned and no data underutilized.

Municipalities must push the limits of their creativity and limited resources to maintain the critical infrastructures inherent in our cities, towns and villages globally. Large scale and depth of complexity are major barriers to solving smart city challenges relating to road infrastructure and asset management. Add the challenges of a 'resource-scarce' COVID-19 environment, and municipal leaders need to find ways to automate work, which in this case are mostly manual road inspection patrols and legacy public works processes. They also need to manage core infrastructure assets, analyze data for capital planning and utilize data analytics for building strategic asset management policies. All of which are expected to result in higher levels of service, better community engagement and more prudent use of taxpayer dollars. For all of this to happen, smart cities' vast data pools collected, processed and turned into actionable data.

People use tools to solve problems and quantum computing is merely another tool. An incredibly fast processing tool that will change the face of so many industries in the future, much like artificial intelligence is doing today.

How are AI & QC changing/will change the face of Asset Management and Road Infrastructure? Three ways. Traffic Flow, Road Construction, and Road Network Maintenance. Let's consider traffic flow.

Traffic Flow

What is the size of the traffic congestion problem? Let's consider the case of one country – Japan. In that country, annual economic losses derived from nationwide traffic congestion, according to an estimate by the Ministry of Land, Infrastructure, Transport, and Tourism (MLIT), totals 12 trillion yen. Whether due to construction, accidents or vehicle distancing, the problem is massive, for both the economy and the environment.

The transportation sector is looking at quantum computing to make traffic management and public transport systems more efficient and ease congestion. Devices like drones, sensors, cameras, robots, self-driving vehicles, traffic signals and others collect data every day on traffic flow in an inhabited area. Instead of using all that data to assess one option at a time, quantum computers can simultaneously assess a multitude of options, reducing the overall time to solution. Traffic flow optimization through quantum computing will result in time, cost and energy improvements

Case in point, Volkswagen (VW) is working on "mobility of the future, computer-based optimization to make life easier for people in a digitized city." Together VW and D-Wave, a Canadian quantum computing company have run several traffic and travel pilot optimization programs in locations including Beijing, Barcelona and Lisbon. Bus fleets in Lisbon leveraged QC determined routes using real-time traffic flow data. Traffic flow optimization through quantum computing will result in time, cost and energy improvements.

A Japanese-based experiment with researchers from Toyota Central R&D Labs, University of Tokyo and D-Wave found "results of experiments using a large city consisting of 50×50 intersections show that the proposed method achieves high quality signal operation, compared with the results of a conventional local control method.

Road Construction

Today's reality for determining what's underneath a potential road surface is the time-consuming and costly method of exploratory digging. Collaborations of entities in the future will preface major road construction projects by deploying quantum gravity sensors to permit surveyors to map underground structures. Gathering more accurate and detailed data through such sensors, and transmitting them to be processed by a quantum computer, should offer faster, more significant insights into terrain, depths, layers, composition and more.

New technologies promise to help municipalities better manage urban environments and deliver services more effectively and efficiently. They can help to make communities more liveable, sustainable, and fair. Many involve the collection and use of large amounts of information, including personal data.

Cities or municipalities that use these connected technologies are often described as "smart cities" according to The Office of the Information and Privacy Commissioner of Ontario, or IPC.

Organizations that begin planning the use of quantum computing will have a substantial advantage over those who rely solely on classical computing infrastructures.

Road Network Maintenance

One of the emerging smart cities is the City of Guelph, who tasked IRIS R&D Group Inc. (IRIS), to develop a solution that will allow the City to improve the capture, monitoring, analysis, and forecasting of information related to the quality of the road network. IRIS is leveraging artificial intelligence to help Guelph achieve these goals. Where artificial intelligence may not be adequate, quantum computing promises to be a more exciting and robust solution.

In terms of road network maintenance, IRIS's work with the City of Guelph seeks to deploy its dashcam technology to a massive data-gathering effort. IRIS's dashcam integrates AI technology to detect road deficiencies and collects actionable data to prioritize work in cities. Together, the City and the company "push the iPORT ™ Dash cam technology to identify deficiencies. Dashcams could open preventative maintenance opportunities and shift decisions that can prolong the lifecycle of the City's roads."

So, can solutions like IRIS' AI-powered technology be augmented by quantum computing in the future? Given quantum computing's application to traffic flow optimization and construction, what about those road network maintenance demands? As a straight optimization problem, road surfacing and replacement could be organized on a system-wide scale then executed on a street-street basis. Municipal transportation leaders would want to understand if QC can help develop new road materials? Can traffic flow be optimized for minimizing road degradation through QC? Can fleet trucks be upgraded to reduce road wear? Can QC help municipalities address road wear by accelerating observation of damage and issuing guidance to maintenance crews before damage is critical? The answer to these questions remains to be seen; however, the problems for which we might apply quantum technology have correlations to traffic flow and road construction as well.

Chapter 18

Quantum in the Future

"Prepare yourself for a wild and fascinating journey – and it all starts with a qubit" – Jay Gambetta and Jerry Chow (IBM Thomas J Watson Research Center)

When will we no longer be able to validate quantum computing results on a classical computer? Honeywell says as soon as 2023. Today, in order to demonstrate that results from a quantum computer are accurate, users can compare notes by running the data on a CPU or GPU. Yet soon classical computers won't be able to keep up says the manufacturer of the H1 quantum computer.

We have so many questions about the future of quantum computing:

- When will we reach 1 million qubits and 10,000 qubit volume?
- When will a quantum computer be the size of a laptop?
- When will the cost of a quantum computer be low enough for the average computer user?
- When will classical computing be replaced or will it ever?

- Which type of quantum computing will reign supreme?
- When will there be a universal fault tolerant quantum computer?

Before publishing this book, I created and launched a LinkedIn poll asking the question "Will Quantum Computing Be Commercially Viable Within ... 1 year, 5 years or 10 years". The results? 8% believed in quantum computing's maturity in 1 year. 74% thought it was five years. The remaining 18% felt quantum computing would mature to commercial viability within 10 years. While not scientific or statistically significant, the poll illustrates the difference in attitudes and perceptions toward quantum computing's maturity. My view is that quantum maturity will evolve much like classical computing and artificial intelligence has over time. Progressive discoveries in parallel with commercial, academic and government immediate uses to continue the public and private funding ecosystem.

Quantum computing for business, as I have argued within this book, is not about perfection. It is about improvement and contribution to business goals. Many companies like D-Wave, QCWare and IDQuantique are focused on immediate benefit to their clients. Performing computations and arriving at the same response as classical computing is still a benefit, especially when a client is waiting for a faster price quote, distribution solution, or drug discovery.

Quantum technology is about speed, accuracy, qubit stability and problem complexity. One of the major quantum-related headlines of 2020 was IBM sharing its roadmap through 2023 when it would achieve a 1,000 qubit (between 10 and 50 logical or usable qubits) machine. It's unlikely organizations or groups of organizations will take an Apollo program approach where a collective of individuals work for a decade for a breakthrough moment. The way quantum is progressing is through daily discoveries and adjustments to the technology.

The universal fault tolerant quantum computer (UFTQ) is still predicted to be years away, yet waiting for perfection makes little sense. Quantum technology will evolve in increments and remain commercially viable pending that UFTQ computer. Compact quantum sensors like the ones being developed at the University of Amsterdam, collaborations like Quantum Industry Canada, QEDC and QUIC, large scale quantum infrastructure network deployment like that begun in China, convergence of technologies, space travel and atomic clocks, teleportation – the future is full of opportunities and certainly its script is not written yet.

From 2021 forward, Stephane Nappo, Vice President, Global Chief Information Security Officer at Groupe SEB, foresees five key predictions for quantum computing; "Quantum innovation will expand, increasing science, systems, and design. Coding methodology for quantum computing will further evolve. Artificial Intelligence to the rescue! The cybersecurity sector will benefit from Quantum Computing power and limitless opportunity in detection, reaction, mitigation and real time monitoring of low signals, abnormalities, fraud attempts, intrusions! The challenges of moving to new cryptographic infrastructures will be recognised and understood better. Programmers will concentrate on quantum-safe cryptography. China's quantum technology might rise to a world-leading position."

What do you think of Mr. Nappo's list? I realize that quantum computing is not exactly mainstream technology. Some believe it to be years, or decades away. Yet, every day I read 5 or more articles about the topic and see developments in quantum computing accelerate. Don't be surprised if by this time next year, we'll be talking about quantum computing much like we do about artificial intelligence today.

What about quantum teleportation? NASA scientist and partners are busy investigating the phenomenon today and have achieved for the first time, "sustained, high-fidelity 'quantum teleportation' of instant transfer of 'qubits', the basic unit of quantum information… with fidelity greater than 90%" over a fibre-optic network 44 kilometers (27 miles). What does that mean for things larger than a qubit in future? Inanimate objects being teleported? People? Very 'Star Trek' transporter-like.

"SpaceX SN15 Stuck the Landing!" That was the title of a popular post I wrote in May 2021 after the incredible milestone was achieved by SpaceX in landing their massive Starship, the vehicle destined for Moon and Mars landings. In terms of the future of space travel, quantum computing will play a vital role in spatial positioning, optimization, logistics, maintenance, weather forecasting, fuel research and more.

One day, in the not too distant future quantum computers will be revolutionizing the way we compute, the way we interact, the way we communicate, move and live. Technology like artificial intelligence and quantum computing is racing forward. Which means the learning curve is accelerated and those who are pioneering will be leaping ahead.

In the future, coordination and collaboration will be a major factor in the advance of quantum computing. Groups like QEDC, QUIC, Quantum Industry Canada and others working together to streamline investments and converge towards optimal technological solutions. Vendors, manufacturers and develops have already begun to team up, bringing their own expertise to a quantum project and that approach will continue.

Hybrid solvers (combinations of classical computers and their quantum brethren) will continue to play a very active part in complex problems like optimizations and simulations playing to the strengths of each technology in scale, speed and processing power. Quantum computing performance and scale are forecast to increase rapidly.

The multitude of quantum technologies today – we described eight of them in this book – should converge to some degree in the next decade with implications like cost, processing speed, temperature requirements, size, green energy impacts, customer preferences and more come into play.

Circuit capability will expand dramatically over the next decade. Today IBM executes a billion quantum circuits a day from external parties. That number will increase a thousand-fold to trillions of quantum circuits being run on futuristic hardware through the cloud.

Quantum error rates (today around 1% according to IBM) are forecast to reduce to the 0.0001% to 0.0005% within just a few years, giving decision makers greater confidence in this relatively new technology.

Standardization of quantum is expected to be driven by organizations like the US National Institute for Standards and Technology. Algorithm developers will call for their own standardization whether that be a Qiskit model (the open-source quantum computing software development kit) or some other. Questions of ethics and responsibility in the use of quantum computing will be raised much like has been done over the past decade with artificial intelligence.

Governments around the world will continue to invest in research, development, supporting collaborations in academia and industry, in the billions of dollars whether through earlier announcement or those pending. Global leadership in quantum computing and its power will create a quantum race for the optimal solutions and first in place recognition and standards.

While the quantum cryptography effort continues (and quantum cryptography will eventually replace the classical RSA-type security), post-quantum cryptography will begin to take precedence in the next decade as quantum computer faces quantum computer in the security forum. Watch, in particular, the NIST's competition for a quantum cryptography standard due to be decided upon in 2022 and the QKD method being deployed today.

What is easier to predict is the need for organizations to start today in developing internal talent, vendor relationships, including quantum in their business priorities, and that a current 500 vendor ecosystem will continue to grow globally. Vendors developing and publishing their own roadmaps to bring their partners along for the ride. Like any other industry, consolidation is on the table as well. In fact, Chirag Dekate of Gartner says "Over the next few years, we see the potential for consolidation of some of these around a core set of providers."

Academic institutions will begin to understand the importance of this ubiquitous technology and how new roles will evolve that require at a minimum of a basic understanding of quantum physics, quantum applications for business, and the worldwide quantum ecosystem to support their organization's goals will into the future. Learning all of these elements do not require a PhD. The most successful academic institutions will offer courses in common language for an otherwise complex subject.

CEO's and CTO's need to continue to focus on their core activities – that does not change with quantum computing. What does change for C-Suite leadership is the introduction of a new technology that will open your business to new ways to solve your most complex problems. How can you ignore that path, when your competition will be running that direction? Quantum computing exists in practical applications today. JP Morgan Chase, Royal Bank, Goldman Sachs, municipalities like Tokyo, Lisbon and Sydney, pharma companies and the military are all investing today and leveraging the technology. Quantum computing is not a fad, or a technology ready for a 'winter' like AI experienced a number of times through history. Your leadership team needs to be ready to position your organization to leverage quantum computing.

Chapter 19

Conclusion

"The 100-qubit quantum computer will not change the world right away—[but] we should regard it as a significant step toward the more powerful quantum technologies of the future"
Dr. John Preskill

Today is merely a point in time. You have a phenomenal opportunity to leverage the power of quantum computing as it matures to achieve your organizational goals. As John Preskill says in the quote above, the first generation of quantum computers may not change the world, but that's not likely your goal. Your success will depend upon your motivation, knowledge, use of technology, and how that technology evolves.

The journey that I have been on for the last four years taught me to think about quantum computing in two distinct ways. One, simply, as a tool – one which can be leveraged in a myriad of ways. Two, a complex science that even Richard Feynman argued was too difficult to completely understand. My journey was fraught with challenges, milestones, technology purchases, research, heated discussions, and a good deal of sweat. It was worth every step. But you can shorten that journey through this book.

You bought this book to achieve some goal. Possibly to be more competitive, to support your customer journey, or to drive new discoveries. Whichever the reason, I hope reading this book will help you on your way. I am so passionate about quantum computing's possibilities and potential and I'm learning something new every day. I'm pushing myself to be curious, to learn, to collaborate and to share my view of quantum computing with as wide an audience as possible.

For those who wish to dive deeper on any topic presented in this book, there are over 35 pages of reference materials to scan and discover and dozens of definitions, names of industry players, and more. The world of quantum computing is just beginning and as a business leader or professional, you should know there is no shortage of resources to learn what you need to about this relatively new technology and supercharge your business.

By reading this book, you've demonstrated, at a minimum, your openness to the potential of quantum computing in the world of business. If you've read this far, continue reading from other sources. Make it part of your everyday activities. There is so much to know about quantum computing, and it's accelerating daily. Find ways to keep current, and it will pay dividends. Buckle your seat belt for what will be an incredible ride.

Brian Lenahan, Mississauga, Canada 2021

A Quick Favor Please?

Before you go may I ask you for a quick favor?
Good, I knew I could count on you.

Would you please leave this book a review on Amazon?

Reviews are very important for authors, as they help us sell more books. This will in turn enable me to write more books for you.

Please take a quick minute to go to Amazon and leave this book an honest review. I promise it doesn't take very long, but it can help this book reach more readers just like you.

Thank you for reading and thank you so much for being part of the journey.
-Brian

Brian Lenahan is an Artificial Intelligence and Quantum Computing Strategist whose Artificial Intelligence training took place at the Massachusetts Institute of Technology (MIT) Sloan School of Management (Cambridge, MA) and Quantum Computing training through CERN and TU Delft University. During a 22-year career, including executive roles at a Fortune 500 Bank in US and Canada, his consistent career thread has been aligning technology & business needs.

Leading multimillion-dollar programs, and teams of over 150 employees in the US, Canada and partnering with resources in India, Brian understands the demands of leadership. He has experience in numerous industries including Financial Services, Computer Services, Transportation, and Real Estate as well as functions including Strategy, IT, HR, Operations, Learning, and Financial Crimes & Fraud Management. He has consulted to C-Suite and Senior Management leaders for over 15 years.

Brian Lenahan is a recognized global keynote speaker and a developer of AI & QC strategies for large corporations and scaling firms. He is the CEO of Aquitaine Innovation Advisors (an AI & QC consulting firm) and the AI Advisor at Haltech Regional Innovation Centre based in Burlington, Canada. Brian's experience skydiving, parasailing, zip lining canyons, and running half-marathons led to his personal approach of balancing prudent risk-taking while still seeking out commercial opportunities.

Brian is currently pursuing his Doctorate in Innovation & Strategy and is the author of four previous books on artificial intelligence, Amazon bestseller "Artificial Intelligence: Foundations for Business Leaders and Consultants", "Digital Coach: Coaching in the Era of Artificial Intelligence", and "Artificial Intelligence: Transitions – How to Successfully Prepare for Career Where AI is Everywhere", and "Deep Health: Using Artificial Intelligence to Live Longer and Healthier" all available on Amazon.ca. He is also an Instructor at McMaster University in Hamilton, Ontario, Canada.

APPENDICES

Glossary

Author's Note: Since definitions must be highly specific and accurate, the following terms and their definitions are taken directly from the sources identified in the 'Notes' section of this book.

Absolute Zero — Absolute zero is the lowest temperature that is theoretically possible, at which the motion of particles that constitutes heat would be minimal. It is zero on the Kelvin scale, equivalent to –273.15°C or –459.67°F. In order to increase stability, most quantum computing systems operate at temperatures near absolute zero.

Adiabatic quantum computer – Operating at 0 Kelvin, this is an idealized quantum computer with similar computational power as gate-based quantum computers.

Algorithm — An algorithm is the specification of a precise set of instructions that can be mechanically applied to yield the solution to any given instance of a problem. A specific approach, often described in mathematical terms, used by a computer to solve a certain problem or carry out a certain task.

Analog - A computer whose operation is based on analog signals and that does not use Boolean logic operations and does not reject noise. A quantum computer that carries out a computation without breaking the operations down to a small set of primitive operations (gates) on qubits; there is currently no model of full fault tolerance for such machines. An analog signal is one whose value varies smoothly within a range of real or complex numbers.

Classical computer: The traditional form of binary digital electronic computing device, almost always running on silicon semiconductor transistor and integrated-circuit hardware.

Coherence—The quality of a quantum system that enables quantum phenomena such as interference, superposition, and entanglement. Mathematically speaking, a quantum system is coherent when the complex coefficients of the contributing quantum states are clearly defined in relation to each other, and the system can be expressed in terms of a single wave function.

Coherence Time — Coherence time is the length of time a quantum superposition state can survive.

Computational complexity—The difficulty of carrying out a specific computational task, typically expressed as a mathematical expression that reflects how the number of steps required to complete the task varies with the size of the input to the problem.

Decoherence—A process where a quantum system will ultimately exchange some energy and information with the broader environment over time, which cannot be recovered once lost. This process is one source of error in qubit systems. Mathematically speaking, decoherence occurs when the relationship between the coefficients of a quantum system's contributing states become ill-defined.

Digital quantum computer—A quantum system where the computation is done by using a small set of primitive operations, or gates, on qubits.

Dilution refrigerator—A specialized cooling device capable of maintaining an apparatus at temperatures near absolute zero.

Distance—In an error-correcting code, the number of bit errors that would be required to convert one valid state of a computer to another. When the number of errors is less than (D–1)/2, one can still extract the error-free state.

Doped Diamonds — A doped diamond is one into which a defect has been intentionally added. Physicists have discovered that they can make good use of these defects to manipulating the spin of quantum particles.

Entanglement — Entanglement is a physical phenomenon that occurs when pairs or groups of particles are generated or interact in ways such that the quantum state of each particle cannot be described independently. If you think that is difficult to understand, you're not alone. Albert Einstein referred to this phenomenon as "spooky action at a distance."

Error-corrected quantum computer—An instance of a quantum computer that emulates an ideal, fault-tolerant quantum computer by running a quantum error correction algorithm.

Exponential speedup: The real case for QCs comes when they provide an exponential speedup, as is the case for certain problems such as breaking public key encryption or simulating chemical and biological systems. If a classical machine would take nine billion years to crack a public key by brute force, a quadratic speedup that reduces the calculation time to 3 billion years is not useful. But an exponential speedup that cracks the code in minutes, or even seconds, is potentially transformative. However, it is unclear just how often QCs will be able to offer exponential speedups. Only a small number of problems are known today where QCs would offer exponential speedups, but optimists note that more will become known over time.

'Fault-tolerant' Material —Fault tolerant materials are a unique class of advanced materials that are electrically insulating on the inside but conducting on the surface. Inducing high-temperature superconductivity on the surface of a topological insulator opens the door to the creation of a pre-requisite for fault-tolerant quantum computing. One of those materials is graphene. Interestingly, the edges of graphene basically turn it into a kind of topological insulator that could be used in quantum computers.

Fidelity – a measure of the quality of hardware operation often calculated as the probability of accuracy.

Logical qubit: A logical qubit uses multiple unreliable physical qubits to produce one reliable logical qubit that is both fault-tolerant and error-corrected. As of 2018, no one has built a logical qubit. The assumption is that a large number of physical qubits will be required to make a logical qubit; the current consensus is that hundreds or even thousands of physical qubits will be required. Large numbers of logical qubits are necessary for a universal or general QC that can solve a wide range of problems. Logical qubit—An abstraction that describes a collection of physical qubits implementing quantum error correction in order to carry out a fault-tolerant qubit operation.

Noisy Intermediate Scale Quantum (NISQ) computing: Although a device composed of hundreds of logical qubits is the ultimate goal, devices with large numbers of physical qubits are likely to have some commercially interesting uses.

These could be thought of as single-task QCs or simulators. A quantum computer that is not error-corrected, but is stable enough to effectively carry out a computation before the system loses coherence. A NISQ can be digital or analog.

Physical qubit: Any two-level quantum-mechanical system can be used as a qubit. These systems include, but are not limited to, photons, electrons, atomic nuclei, atoms, ions, quantum dots, and superconducting electronic circuits. As of 2018, most large QCs use either superconducting qubits or trapped ion technologies.

Gate—A computational operation that takes in and puts out one or more bits (in the case of a classical computer) or qubits (in the case of a quantum computer).

Logic gate—In classical computing, a collection of transistors that input and output digital signals, and that can be represented and modeled using Boolean logic (rules that combine signals that can be either false, 0, or true, 1).

Measurement—Observation of a quantum system, which yields only a single classical output and collapses the system's wave function onto the corresponding state.

Microprocessor—An integrated circuit that contains the elements of a central processing unit on a single chip.

Noise—Unwanted variations in a physical system that can lead to error and unwanted results.

Noise immunity—The ability to remove noise (unwanted variations) in a signal to minimize error.

One-way functions—Functions that are easy to compute in one direction while being for all intents and purposes impossible to compute in the other direction.

Program—An abstraction that refers to the sequence of instructions and rules that a computer must perform to complete one or more tasks (or solve one or more tasks) using a specific approach, or algorithm.

Quantum annealer—An analog quantum computer that operates through coherent manipulation of qubits by changing the analog values of the system's Hamiltonian, rather than by using quantum gates. A quantum annealer performs computations by preparing a set of qubits in some initial state and changing their energy environment until it defines the parameters of a given problem, such that the final state of the qubits corresponds, with a high probability, to the answer of the problem. In general, a quantum annealer is not necessarily universal—there are some problems that it cannot solve.

Quantum information science—The study of how information is or can be encoded in a quantum system, including the associated statistics, limitations, and unique affordances of quantum mechanics.

Quantum interference—When states contributing to coherent superpositions combine constructively or destructively, like waves, with coefficients adding or subtracting.

Quadratic speedup: There are certain computational problems, such as searching an unordered list[i], where a QC would outperform a classical computer by a quadratic amount: If it takes a classical computer N steps to run the process, the QC can do it in √N. (Grover's algorithm is the most famous example of a technique that QCs could use to show a quadratic speedup.) For example, if a given calculation would take 365 days on a classical computer, it would take only 19.1 days on a QC. However, there are few real-world computing tasks done today that take a year, so it is more realistic to say that, if a computation takes eight hours on a classical machine, then it could be done in less than three hours on a QC. That may be a big enough speedup to justify using a quantum computer that costs millions of dollars and requires specialists to run and program it … or it might not. The business case for using a QC when the speedup is only quadratic is not always compelling.

Quantum advantage: Although quantum supremacy is an important theoretical milestone, it is possible that it will be for a computing problem that is of no or little practical importance. Therefore, many believe that quantum advantage will be the more important breakthrough: when a quantum computer can perform a certain useful task that no classical computer can solve in a practical amount of time or using a practical amount of resources

Quantum computer (QC): A computer that uses quantum-mechanical phenomena, such as superposition and entanglement, to perform its calculations. Various (more than 10) contending physical implementations are being tried, many of which require ultra-low temperatures. It is not clear at this time which physical implementation will triumph. Quantum computers are not better than classical computers at everything; they can offer spectacular speedups for certain tasks, but do no better at others, or could even be worse.

Quantum Contextuality — Quantum contextuality is a phenomenon necessary for the “magic” behind universal quantum computation. Physicists have long known that measuring things at the quantum level establishes a state that didn’t exist before the measurement. In other words, what you measure necessarily depends on how you carried out the observation – it depends on the 'context' of the experiment. Scientists at the Perimeter Institute for Theoretical Physics have discovered that this context is the key to unlocking the potential power of quantum computation.

Quantum Logic Gates — In quantum computing and specifically the quantum circuit model of computation, a quantum gate (or quantum logic gate) is a basic quantum circuit operating on a small number of qubits. They are the building blocks of quantum circuits, like classical logic gates are for conventional digital circuits. Quantum logic gates are represented by unitary matrices. The most common quantum gates operate on spaces of one or two qubits, just like the common classical logic gates operate on one or two bits. This means that as matrices, quantum gates can be described by 2×2 or 4×4 unitary matrices. Quantum gates are usually represented as matrices. A gate which acts on k qubits is represented by a 2k x 2k unitary matrix. The number of qubits in the input and output of the gate have to be equal.

Quantum Memory State — Quantum Memory State is the state in which qubits much sustain themselves in order to be of value in quantum computing. To date, these states have proved extremely fragile because the least bit of interference at the quantum level can destroy them. For this reason, most experiments with qubits require particles to be cooled to near absolute zero as well as heavy shielding.

Quantum Register — A collection of n qubits is called a quantum register of size n.

Quantum sensing and metrology—The study and development of quantum systems whose extreme sensitivity to environmental disturbances can be exploited to measure important physical properties with more precision than is possible with classical technologies.

Quantum simulation: The subjects of certain problems, such as chemical processes, molecular dynamics, and the electronic properties of materials, are quantum systems. Classical computers are notoriously ill-suited to performing simulations of quantum systems, and they must rely on crude approximations. Since QCs are also governed by the rules of quantum mechanics, they are well-suited to performing efficient simulations of other quantum systems.

Quantum supremacy or superiority: Both terms are used interchangeable to denote the point at which a quantum computer will be able to perform a certain task that no classical computer can execute in a practical amount of time or using a practical amount of resources. It is critical to note that just because a QC has demonstrated supremacy for one problem does not mean that it is superior for all other—or even any other—problems. There are different degrees by which a QC can provide speeds greater than a classical computer (see the below entries on quadratic and exponential speedups).

Quantum system – An assemblage of minute physical objects which classical physics cannot approximate.

Qubit — A quantum bit or qubit operates in the weirdly wonderful world of quantum mechanics. At that level, subatomic particles can exist in multiple states at once. This is multi-state capability is called superposition. One commonly used particle is the electron, and state normally used to generate a superposition is spin (spin up could represent a "0" and spin down could represent a "1". Additional qubits can be added by a process called entanglement. Theoretically, each extra entangled qubit doubles the number of parallel operations that can be carried out. MIT's Seth Lloyd notes, "We could map the whole Universe — all of the information that has existed since the Big Bang — onto 300 qubits." Qubit—A quantum bit, the fundamental hardware component of a quantum computer, embodied by a quantum object. Analogous to a classical bit (or binary digit), a qubit can represent a state corresponding to either zero or one; unlike a classical bit, a qubit can also exist in a superposition of both states at once, with any possible relative contribution of each. In a quantum computer, qubits are generally entangled, meaning that any qubit's state is inextricably linked to the state of the other qubits, and thus cannot be defined independently.

Run time—The amount of time required to carry out a computational task. In practice, the actual time required for a task depends heavily on the design of a device and of its physical embodiment, so run time may be described in terms of the number of computational steps.

Shor's algorithm — Developed by Peter Shor in 1994, this quantum algorithm could break the encryption protecting Internet communications and data, were it installed on a large-scale quantum computer.

Signal—An electromagnetic field used to convey information in an electronic circuit.

Spin — Spin sometimes called "nuclear spin" or "intrinsic spin" is the quantum version form of angular momentum carried by elementary particles, composite particles (hadrons), and atomic nuclei. Having said that, the website Ask a Mathematician/Ask a Physicist states,

“Spin has nothing to do with actual spinning. … Physicists use the word ‘spin’ or ‘intrinsic spin’ to distinguish the angular momentum that particles ‘just kinda have’ from the regular angular momentum of physically rotating things.”
Superposition — Superposition is an ambiguous state in which a particle can be both a “0” and a “1”.
Topological Qubit — Topological qubits rely on a rare and extraordinarily finicky quantum state; however, once formed, they theoretically would behave like sturdy knots — resistant to the disturbances that wreck the delicate properties of every other kind of qubit.

Superposition—A quantum phenomenon where a system is in more than one state at a time. Mathematically speaking, the wave function of a quantum system in a superposition state is expressed as the sum of the contributing states, each weighted by a complex coefficient.

Scalable, fault-tolerant, universal gate-based quantum computer—A system that operates through gate-based operations on qubits, analogous to circuit-based classical computers, and uses quantum error correction to correct any system noise (including errors introduced by imperfect control signals, or unintended coupling of qubits to each other or to the environment) that occurs during the time frame of the calculation.

Surface code—A quantum error correction code (QECC) that is less sensitive to noise than other established QECCs, but has higher overheads.

Transmon — A transmon is a superconducting loop-shaped qubit that can be created at extremely low temperatures and, at the moment, up to five of them can be linked together. A standard transmon can maintain its coherence for around 50 microseconds – long enough to be used in quantum circuits. What's more, coherence times twice that length, and transmon arrays of 10 to 20 loops, are supposedly just around the corner.

Universal computer—A computer that can perform any computation that could be performed by a Turing machine.

Wave function—A mathematical description of the state of a quantum system, so named to reflect their wave-like characteristics.

Wave-particle duality—The phenomenon where a quantum object is sometimes best described in terms of wave-like properties and sometimes in terms of particle-like properties.

Xmon — An Xmon is a cross-shaped qubit created by a team at the University of California, Santa Barbara. The team found that by placing five Xmons in a single row (with each qubit talking to its nearest neighbor) they were able to create a stable and effective quantum arrangement that provides the most stability and fewest errors. Like most other qubits, the Xmon must be created at temperatures approaching absolute zero.

Security Glossary

Asymmetric cryptography (also public key cryptography)—A category of cryptography where the system uses public keys that are widely known and private keys that are secret to the owner; such systems are commonly used for key exchange protocols in the encryption of most of today's electronic communications.

Certificate authority—An entity that issues a digital certificate to certify the ownership of a public key used in online transactions.

Cipher—An approach to concealing the meaning of information by encoding it.

Ciphertext—The encrypted form of a message, which appears scrambled or nonsensical.

Classical attack—An attempt by a classical computer to break or subvert encryption.

Cryptography—The study and practice of encoding information to obfuscate its content that relies upon the difficulty of solving certain mathematical problems.

Cryptosystem—A method of deploying a specific cryptographic algorithm to protect data and communications from being read by an unintended recipient.

Decryption algorithm—A set of instructions for returning an encrypted message to its unencrypted form. Such an algorithm takes as input a cipher text and its encryption key, and returns a cleartext, or readable, version of the message.

Digital signature—An important cryptographic mechanism used to verify data integrity.

Encryption—The application of cryptography to protect information, currently widely used in computer systems and Internet communications.

Encryption algorithm—A set of instructions for converting understandable data to an incomprehensible cipher, or ciphertext. In practice, the algorithm takes as input the message to be encrypted along with an encryption key and scrambles the message according to a mathematical procedure.

Key exchange—A step in cryptographic algorithms and protocols where keys are shared among intended recipients to enable their use in encrypting and decrypting information.

Post-quantum cryptography—The set of methods for cryptography that are expected to be resistant to cryptanalysis by a quantum computer.

Quantum cryptography - A subfield of quantum communication where quantum properties are used to design communication systems that may not be eavesdropped upon by an observer.

Symmetric encryption—A type of encryption where a secret key, shared by both the sender and the receiver, is used to encrypt and decrypt communications.

Transport Layer Security (TLS) handshake—The most common key exchange protocol, used to protect Internet traffic.

Appendix

Quantum Vendors – Notable Information From Company Websites

D-Wave Systems Inc.	User-developed early quantum applications on D-Wave systems, including airline scheduling, election modeling, quantum chemistry simulation, automotive design, preventative healthcare, logistics	Annealing
IBM	IBM Quantum Network is currently working with over 119 partners across multiple industries, developing real world commercial applications in chemistry, optimization, risk analysis	Superconducting Qiskit Quantum Lab
Xanadu	• Brings Quantum Machine Learning to customers with Amazon Braket • Canada's first quantum network designed for innovation and collaboration • First photonic quantum computer on the cloud • First quantum computer that can operate at room temperature • BMO Financial Group and Scotiabank Partner with Xanadu on quantum computing speedups for trading products	Photonic
Zapata	Optimization • Sampling from risk-	Bridge between quantum hardware and

	neutral probability measure for asset pricing • Portfolio optimization by quantum annealing or gate-model quantum heuristics • Improved asset allocation by quantum-inspired optimization Simulation & Modeling • Quantum-assisted Monte Carlo for derivative pricing, credit valuation adjustment • Imaginary-time propagation for multi-asset BlackScholes equation • Accelerated sampling from stochastic processes for risk analysis Machine Learning • Improved graph clustering analysis for anomaly and fraud detection • Time series analysis of financial data using quantum Boltzmann machines • Dimensionality reduction for financial data using	software for enterprise

	quantum-classical hybrid optimization	
Honeywell	Applications in: • Pharmaceuticals • Chemical • Finance • Aerospace & Defence • Oil & Gas • Data Centers • Manufacturing • Telecommunications	Ion Trap
CQC	Applications in: • Molecular Simulation • Cybersecurity • Ironbridge encryption • Quantum Machine Learning • Finance	Photonic t|ket software
Rigetti	Developer of quantum integrated circuits used for quantum computers. The company also develops a cloud platform called Forest that enables programmers to write quantum algorithms.	Superconducting

Quantum Computing Industry Players

Name	Title	Company
Brian Martin	Senior Data Scientist & Head of AI in R&D Information Research	AbbVie
Jeremy Sosabowski	CEO and Co-Founder	AlgoDynamix
Richard Moulds	General Manager	Amazon Braket
Eric Kessler	Senior Product Manager, Science	Amazon Web Services
Thomas Monz	Co-Founder & CEO	AQT
David Vettesse	Sales Director	AQT
Brian Lenahan	CEO/Quantum Strategist/AI Advisor Haltech/Author	Aquitaine Innovation Advisors
Xavier Geoffret	HPC & Quantum Global Presales	Atos
Natalia Jimenez	Atos HPC, AI & Quantum Life Sciences Centre of Excellence Director	Atos
Sabine Keravel	Sales Operations	Atos
Philippe Duluc	Chief Technology Officer	Atos
Xavier Vigouroux	Strategic Collaboration Coordinator	Atos
Brian Standen	Global Head of Next Generation Computing	BASF
Thomas Park	VP strategic Initiatives & Operations	BDC Capital
David Gunnarsson	Chief Sales Officer & Principal Scientist	Bluefors
Elvira Shishenina	Quantum Computing Research & Applications Lead	BMW Group
Oliver Wick	Technology Scout & Futurist	BMW Group
Johannes Klepsch	Product Owner Quantum Computing	BMW Group
Tobias Jahn	Principal	BMW iVentures
Elica Kyoseva	Quantum Computing Scientist	Boehringer Ingelheim
Jay Lowell	Chief Engineer, Senior Technical Fellow, Disruptive Computing & Networks	Boeing
Rodolfo Bonnin	Co-innovation Data Engineer	Bonzzu
Clena Abuan	Senior Technology Associate	BP
Corneliu Buda	Molecular Modeler	BP
Richard Debney	VP Digital Science	BP
Julianna Toms	Technology Principal	BP
Eric Doskocil	Expert Scientist	BP
Andrew Lord	Senior Manager, Optical Research	BT

Dr. Simon McAdams	Quantum Chemistry Product Lead	Cambridge Quantum Computing
Mark Jackson	Quantum Evangelist	Cambridge Quanutm Computing
Duncan Jones	Head of Quantum Cybersecurity	Cambridge Quanutm Computing
Edward Chiu	Cybersecurity Strategist & Distinguished Engineer	Chevron
Santanu Ganguly	Systems Architect	Cisco Systems
Nir Minerbi	CEO	Classiq
Yehuda Naveh	CTO	Classiq
Morgan Polotan	Principal	Comcast Ventures & Genacast Ventures
Christian Gologin	Expert Advanced Computational Concepts and Quantum Computing	Covestro
Christian Gogolin	Expert Advanced Computational Concepts and Quantum Computing	Covestro AG
Jennifer Houston	SVP Marketing and Public Affairs	D-Wave Systems
Andy Edmonds	Principal Scientist	Element Six
Matthew Markham	Senior Scientist	Element Six
Daniel Twitchen	Chief Technologist	Element Six
Salman Al Jimeely	Director	Elyah
Joydip Gosh	Quantum Computing Lead	Ford Motor Co.
Matt Trevithick	COO, Google Quantum AI	Google
Tony Uttley	President of Honeywell Quantum Solutions -	Honeywell
Gustavo Ordonez-Sanz	Quantum Computing Lead	HSBC
Joseph Broz	VP, Quantum Growth & Market Development	IBM
Dr. Bruno Huttner	Director of Strategic Quantum Initiatives, and Quantum Key Distribution Expert	ID Quantique
Dr. Amin Abbasi	Business Development Manager	imec
Sinisha Patkovic	Managing Director, EMEA	ISARA
Dominic Widdows	Senior Principal NLP Scientist	LivePerson
Darren Brock	Principal Research Engineer, Space	Lockheed Martin Corporation
Marco Cerezo-	Quantum Information Theorist	Los Alamos National Labs
Steve Flinter	Vice President, Artificial Intelligence & Machine Learning	Mastercard Labs
Ivan Ostojic	Partner	Mckinsey & Company
Rodney Zemmel	Global Leader, McKinsey Digital	Mckinsey & Company

Hans Melo	CEO	MentenAl
Kam Chana	Director, Scientific Modeling Programs	Merck
Thomas Ehmer	Business Technologies R&D	Merck KGA
Matthias Troyer	Distinguished Scientist & Director of Quantum Customer Solutions	Microsoft
Anne Marie Engtoft Larsen	Tech Ambassador	Ministry of Foreign Affairs, Denmark
Pedro Costa	Managing Director, Global Head of Data Science & Analytics, CCIB	Morgan Stanley
Matt Cashia	Vice President	Morgan Stanley
Samuel Mugel	Co-Founder	Multiverse Computing
Tatjana Wilk	General Manager	Munich Center for Quantum Science and Technology
Rupak Biswas	Director of Exploration Technology	NASA
Dustin Moody	Mathematician, Cryptographic Technology Group	NIST
Carl Williams	Acting Director, Physical Measurement Laboratory	NIST (National Institute of Standards & Technology)
Elena Boto	Research Fellow	Nottingham University
Yoshihisa Yamamoto	Director of the PHI (Physics & Informatics) Laboratories	NTT Research, Inc.
Carmen Palacios-Berraquero	Co-Founder & CEO	Nu Quantum
Matthew Versaggi -	Senior Director of Artificial Intelligence & Cognitive Technology	Optum
Professor Tommaso Calarco	Director / Coordinator	Peter Grunberg Institute, EU Quantum Flagship
Vassilios Pantazopoulos	Head of Scientific Computing & HPC	Pfizer
Peter Shadbolt	Chief Scientist	PsiQuantum
Dr. Niels Bultink	Co-Founder & CEO	Qblox
Yianni Gamvros	Head of Business Development	QC Ware
Rob Parrish	Head of Chemistry Simulations	QC Ware
Rob Parrish	Head of Chemistry Simulations	QC Ware
Jonatan Kutchinsky	CEO & Co-Founder	QDevil
James Nguyen	CEO and Co-Founder	Quantropi
Michael Redding	CTO	Quantropi
Doug Finke	Managing Editor	Quantum Computing Report
Freeke Heijman	Founding Director	Quantum Delta NL
Celia Merzbacher	Associate Director	Quantum Economic Development Consortium

Zac Dutton	Lead Scientist	Raytheon BBN Technologies
Hanna Helin	Head of Emerging Technology Strategy	Refinitiv
Marco Magagnini	Partner	Reply Data
Mandy Birch	SVP Technology Partnerships	Rigetti
Mark Field	Principal Scientist	Rigetti
Ruslan Yunusov	Head of Project Office for quantum technologies and National Quantum Lab	Rosatom & National Quantum Lab
Maria Lepskaya	Senior Associate	Runa Capital
Vishal Shete	Head of Quantum Lab	Sia Partners
Karan Pinto -	Senior Venture Builder	Sia Partners
Alexei Kondratyev	Managing Director, Global Head of Data Science & Analytics, CCIB	Standard Chartered Bank
Emir Roach	Director	Takeda
Antonio Manzalini	Senior Project Manager	Telecom Italia Mobile
Ole Kock	Product Development Manager, Quantum	Teledyne e2v
Jon Allcock	Senior Researcher	Tencent Quantum Laboratory
Sheila Rowan CBE	Chief Scientific Advisor for Scotland	The Scottish Government
Maran van Heesch	Quantum Security Expert	TNO
Bhushan Bonde	Head of IT Early Solutions Innovation Development	UCB
Roger McKinlay	Challenge Director, Quantum Technologies	UK Innovation & Research
Sebastian Weidt	CEO & Founder	Universal Quantum
John Martinis	Professor of Physics	University of California, Santa Barbara
Michael Hayduk	Deputy Director, Information Directorate	US Air Force
Alex Kiltz	Principal	UVC Partners
Marc Kaplan	CEO	VeriQloud
Florian Neukart	Director, Data Lab	Volkswagen Group of America
Peter Bordow	SVP & Principal Systems Architect for Advanced Technologies	Wells Fargo
Zachary Vernon	Head of Hardware	Xanadu
Paul Finlay	Quantum Ambassador	Xanadu
Rafal Janik	Head of Product	Xanadu
Christopher Savoie	Founder & CEO	Zapata Computing

NOTES

Introduction

Wired UK. Quantum computing and quantum supremacy, explained. Mar. 4, 2020.
https://www.youtube.com/watch?v=QF7QfE6qgTM

QC Ware. Practical Quantum Computing.
https://q2b.qcware.com

X Corp. Quantum Business Europe.
https://www.quantumbusinesseurope.com

Fadilpašić, Sead. "Majority of decision makers plan to harness quantum computing in near future". ITProPortal. September 30, 2020
https://www.itproportal.com/news/majority-of-decision-makers-plan-to-harness-quantum-computing-in-near-future/

Baines. Stewart. "Quantum computing – next big thing or hype?" February 12, 2019. Orange. https://www.orange-business.com/en/blogs/quantum-computing-next-big-thing-or-hype

Consultancy.uk . "Quantum computing market to reach $1 trillion by 2035". News. 15 April 2020. https://www.consultancy.uk/news/24361/quantum-computing-market-to-reach-1-trillion-by-2035

Chapter 1

IBM Institute for Business Value. "Five strategies to prepare for paradigm-shifting quantum technology" https://www.ibm.com/thought-leadership/institute-business-value/report/quantumstrategy

Walsh, Bryan. "Quantum computing's growing advantage". Axios. Dec. 9, 2020. https://www.axios.com/quantum-advantage-google-china-computing-1f1b66e1-36e4-4329-af54-36d77417474d.html

Lee, Chris. Quantum device performs 2.6 billion years of computation in 4 minutes. Ars Technica. Dec. 7, 2020. https://arstechnica.com/science/2020/12/un-computable-quantum-maze-computed-by-quantum-maze-computer/

Staff. "Hype Cycle for Compute Infrastructure". Gartner. https://www.gartner.com/en/documents/3987268/hype-cycle-for-compute-infrastructure-2020

Staff. Gartner CEO Survey 2021 – Shift in Business Leader Priorities.

http://public2.brighttalk.com/resource/core/339403/may11kmoyersssmithmraskino_743776.pdf

Chapter 2

D-Wave. “D-Wave Announces Promotion of Dr. Alan Baratz to CEO - Chief Product Officer and head of R&D assumes role of Chief Executive Officer.” Intrado Globe Newswire. December 09, 2019. https://www.globenewswire.com/news-release/2019/12/09/1958234/0/en/D-Wave-Announces-Promotion-of-Dr-Alan-Baratz-to-CEO.html

“Building a Quantum Computing startup with Chad Rigetti (Rigetti Computing)” Techcrunch Disrupt SF 2018. September 7, 2018 https://techcrunch.com/video/building-a-quantum-computing-startup-with-chad-rigetti-rigetti-computing-disrupt-sf-2018/

Hsu, Jeremy. “Measuring Progress in the 'Noisy' Era of Quantum Computing”. IEEE Spectrum. 20 Oct 2020 https://spectrum.ieee.org/tech-talk/computing/hardware/measuring-progress-in-the-noisy-era-of-quantum-computing

University of Waterloo Institute for Quantum Computing. “New protocol is a huge breakthrough for the future of quantum computers”. Institute for Quantum Computing News. August 2020. https://uwaterloo.ca/institute-for-quantum-computing/news/new-protocol-huge-breakthrough-future-quantum-computers

Caltech. John Preskill Bio. http://theory.caltech.edu/~preskill/ https://arxiv.org/abs/1801.00862

Wikipedia. Timeline of Quantum Computing. https://en.wikipedia.org/wiki/Timeline_of_quantum_computing_and_communication

Wikipedia. Quantum Noise. https://en.wikipedia.org/wiki/Quantum_noise

Staff. "D-Wave Announces General Availability of First Quantum Computer Built for Business" . Sep. 29, 2020 https://www.dwavesys.com/press-releases/d-wave-announces-general-availability-first-quantum-computer-built-business

Nachman, B., Urbanek, M., de Jong, W.A. *et al.* Unfolding quantum computer readout noise. *npj Quantum Inf* **6,** 84 (2020). https://doi.org/10.1038/s41534-020-00309-7 https://www.nature.com/articles/s41534-020-00309-7

PR Newswire Staff. "Cambridge Quantum Computing Announces Significant New Quantum Technology Collaboration With CERN" Feb 28, 2020. https://www.prnewswire.com/news-releases/cambridge-quantum-computing-announces-significant-new-quantum-technology-collaboration-with-cern-301012905.html

IonQ. "Algorithmic Qubit Calculator". December 9, 2020 https://ionq.com/algorithmic-qubit-calculator

Kelsey, Todd. "Sooner Than We Think? We Spoke with Murray Thom, D-Wave's VP of Product Management, About Production-Ready Quantum Apps". The Quantum Daily. April 25, 2021

https://www.thequantumdaily.com/2021/04/25/sooner-than-we-think-we-spoke-with-murray-thom-d-waves-vp-of-product-management-about-production-ready-quantum-apps/

Staff. "Quantum technologies identified as a major trend for 2020" ID Quantique. https://www.idquantique.com/quantum-technologies-identified-as-a-major-trend-for-2020/

Dowling, Jonathan; Milburn, Gerard. "QUANTUM TECHNOLOGY: THE SECOND QUANTUM REVOLUTION." Arxiv. https://arxiv.org/ftp/quant-ph/papers/0206/0206091.pdf

Chapter 3

Swayne, Matt. "UK-based Quantum Motion Researchers Report They Have Blueprint for Scalable Future in Quantum Computing." The Quantum Daily. April 5, 2021. https://thequantumdaily.com/2021/04/05/uk-based-quantum-motion-researchers-report-they-have-blueprint-for-scalable-future-in-quantum-computing/

Gibney, Elizabeth. "Quantum computer race intensifies as alternative technology gains steam" Nature. Nov. 7, 2020 https://www.nature.com/articles/d41586-020-03237-w

JILA. "Neutral Atom Quantum Computing" 2021. https://jila.colorado.edu/dzanderson/research-area-description/neutral-atom-quantum-computing

Staff. "Wiring a new path to scalable quantum computing". Riken. Jul. 3, 2020 https://www.riken.jp/en/news_pubs/research_news/rr/20200703_2/index.html

Schreiber, Amelie. “What is… a Quantum Circuit Transpiler? Optimizing Quantum Circuits”. Towards Data Science. Dec 22, 2019
https://towardsdatascience.com/what-is-a-quantum-circuit-transpiler-ba9a7853e6f9

Dargan, James. “19 Companies Lighting Up The Quantum Photonics Sector”. The Quantum Daily. February 4, 2021
https://thequantumdaily.com/2021/02/04/19-companies-lighting-up-the-quantum-photonics-sector/

Pezzagna, Sébastien; Meijera, Jan. “Quantum computer based on color centers in diamond” Applied Physics Reviews. 10 February 2021
https://aip.scitation.org/doi/10.1063/5.0007444

Dargan, James. “UGhent Spinoff Discovering The Possibilities of Quantum Dots”. The Quantum Daily. April 9, 2021
https://thequantumdaily.com/2021/04/09/ughent-spinoff-discovering-the-possibilities-of-quantum-dots/

Dargan, James. “10 Companies Providing Full-Stack Quantum Solutions” The Quantum Daily. May 10, 2021.
https://www.thequantumdaily.com/2021/05/09/10-companies-providing-full-stack-quantum-solutions/

Research & Markets. “Global Quantum Dot Market (2020 to 2025) - Key Players Include Samsung Electronics, Nanosys, Nanoco Group & QD Laser Among Others” Globe Newswire. April 09, 2020
https://www.globenewswire.com/news-release/2020/04/09/2014106/0/en/global-quantum-dot-market-2020-to-2025-key-players-include-samsung-electronics-nanosys-nanoco-group-qd-laser-among-others.html

Research & Markets. "Quantum Computing Market by Technology, Infrastructure, Services, and Industry Verticals 2020 – 2025" https://www.researchandmarkets.com/reports/4900662/quantum-computing-market-by-technology?utm_source=dynamic&utm_medium=GNOM&utm_code=n5rjsg&utm_campaign=1341544+-+Global+Quantum+Computing+Market+by+Technology%2c+Infrastructure%2c+Services+and+Industry+Verticals+(2020-2025)&utm_exec=joca220gnomd

PAT Research. What is Quantum Computing? Top 18 Quantum Computing Companies. https://www.predictiveanalyticstoday.com/what-is-quantum-computing/

GCSE Computer Science Revision https://www.computerscience.gcse.guru

Finke, Doug. Private/Startup Companies" Quantum Computing Report. https://quantumcomputingreport.com/privatestartup/

Di Paolo Emilio, Maurizio. "The Future of the Quantum Computing Stack" EE Times. April 10, 2020. https://www.eetimes.com/the-future-of-the-quantum-computing-stack/#

Brooks, Michael. "How a quantum computer actually works Your five-minute guide to how the computers of the future actually operate. Honest."Protocol.com May 4, 2020. https://www.protocol.com/manuals/quantum-computing/how-a-quantum-computer-works

Staff. "U.S. hatches plan to build a quantum Internet that might be unhackable" Washington Post. July 23, 2020. https://www.washingtonpost.com/technology/2020/07/23/us-plan-quantum-internet/?outputType=amp

IBM Institute of Business Value. "Coming soon to your business— Quantum computing". Research Insights. November 2018.
https://www.ibm.com/downloads/cas/OV1V0NLX

Staff. What is Quantum Firmware? Q-CTRL. https://q-ctrl.com/foundations/quantum-firmware/

Orzel, Chad. "What Is A Quantum Computer? The 30,000 Foot Overview" Forbes. Oct 15, 2018
https://www.forbes.com/sites/chadorzel/2018/10/15/what-is-a-quantum-computer-the-30000-foot-overview/#2c40368967bf

Staff. Docs > Qiskit Terra API Reference > Transpiler (qiskit.transpiler)
https://qiskit.org/documentation/apidoc/transpiler.html

Lardinois, Frederic, "IonQ now supports IBM's Qiskit quantum development kit" Techcrunch.com April 12, 2021
https://lnkd.in/gYuTnqa

Staff. "infinityQube, the First Operational Quantum Analog Computer, Is Bringing Quantum Speed to Enterprise" infinity.tech .https://www.infinityq.tech/news

Staff. "What is a Digital Annealer". Fujitsu.
https://www.fujitsu.com/ca/en/services/business-services/digital-annealer/what-is-digital-annealer/

Chapter 4

Staff. "The world's first integrated quantum communication network". phys.org. Retrieved February 11, 2021.

Staff. "Using drones to create local quantum networks". phys.org. Retrieved February 12, 2021.

Staff. “Cancelling quantum noise”. UTS. 23 May 2019 https://www.uts.edu.au/about/faculty-engineering-and-information-technology/news/cancelling-quantum-noise

Staff. "Artificial atoms create stable qubits for quantum computing". phys.org. Retrieved March 9, 2020.

Anderton, Kevin. "The Largest Roadblock In Quantum Computing Has Been Passed [Infographic]". Forbes. Retrieved May 16, 2020.

Staff. “Global Quantum Computing Industry”. PR Newswire. https://markets.businessinsider.com/news/stocks/global-quantum-computing-industry-1029835003

Staff. “The Quantum Computing market is expected to grow from USD 472 million in 2021 to USD 1,765 million by 2026, at a CAGR of 30.2%” Report Linker. Yahoo Finance. https://finance.yahoo.com/news/quantum-computing-market-expected-grow-085400780.html

Staff. “Xi Focus: Xi stresses advancing development of quantum science and technology” Xinhua. 2020-10-18. http://www.xinhuanet.com/english/2020-10/18/c_139448027.htm

Cao,Yudong; Hirzel, Timothy. “Quantum Acceleration in 2020”

https://www.infoq.com/articles/quantum-acceleration-2020/

Katwala, Amit. "Inside big tech's high-stakes race for quantum supremacy" Wired. May 18, 2020.
https://www.wired.co.uk/article/quantum-supremacy-google-microsoft-ibm
"

Staff. NSF establishes 3 new institutes to address critical challenges in quantum information science" National Science Foundation. July 21, 2020
https://www.nsf.gov/news/special_reports/announcements/072120.jsp

Emre, Suresh. "Current state of quantum computing (2019)" August 3, 2019
https://sureshemre.wordpress.com/2019/08/03/current-state-of-quantum-computing-2019/

Galer, Susan. "Quantum Technology 2020 Trends: These Are The Immediate Security Threats And Opportunities." Fortune. Feb 13, 2020
https://www.forbes.com/sites/sap/2020/02/13/quantum-technology-2020-trends-these-are-the-immediate-security-threats-and-opportunities/#5756460e6ac2

Shankland, Stephen. "IBM's biggest-yet 53-qubit quantum computer will come online in October". CNET. Retrieved October 17, 2019.

Staff. "Google may have taken a step towards quantum computing 'supremacy' (updated)". Engadget. Retrieved September 24, 2019.

115th Congress (2018) (June 26, 2018). "H.R. 6227 (115th)". Legislation. GovTrack.us. Retrieved February 11, 2019. National Quantum Initiative Act

Monz, T; Nigg, D; Martinez, E. A; Brandl, M. F; Schindler, P; Rines, R; Wang, S. X; Chuang, I. L; Blatt, R; et al. (March 4, 2016). "Realization of a scalable Shor algorithm". Science. 351 (6277): 1068–1070. arXiv:1507.08852. Bibcode:2016Sci...351.1068M. doi:10.1126/science.aad9480. PMID 26941315. S2CID 17426142.

April 13, 2015 "Breakthrough opens door to affordable quantum computers". Retrieved April 16, 2015.

Córcoles, A.D; Magesan, Easwar; Srinivasan, Srikanth J; Cross, Andrew W; Steffen, M; Gambetta, Jay M; Chow, Jerry M (2015). "Demonstration of a quantum error detection code using a square lattice of four superconducting qubits". Nature Communications. 6: 6979. arXiv:1410.6419. Bibcode:2015NatCo...6.6979C. doi:10.1038/ncomms7979. PMC 4421819. PMID 25923200.

Staff. "D-Wave Systems Inc., the world's first quantum computing company, today announced that it has broken the 1000 qubit barrier". Retrieved June 22, 2015.

October 6, 2015 "Crucial hurdle overcome in quantum computing". Retrieved October 6, 2015.

August 4, 2014 Nemoto, K.; Trupke, M.; Devitt, S. J; Stephens, A. M; Scharfenberger, B; Buczak, K; Nobauer, T; Everitt, M. S; Schmiedmayer, J; Munro, W. J (2014). "Photonic architecture for scalable quantum information processing in diamond". Physical Review X. 4 (3): 031022. arXiv:1309.4277.

Bibcode:2014PhRvX...4c1022N.
doi:10.1103/PhysRevX.4.031022. S2CID 118418371.

Nigg, D; Müller, M; Martinez, M. A; Schindler, P; Hennrich, M; Monz, T; Martin-Delgado, M. A; Blatt, R (July 18, 2014). "Quantum computations on a topologically encoded qubit". Science. 345 (6194): 302–305. arXiv:1403.5426. Bibcode:2014Sci...345..302N. doi:10.1126/science.1253742. PMID 24925911. S2CID 9677048.

Markoff, John. "Scientists Report Finding Reliable Way to Teleport Data". New York Times. Retrieved May 29, 2014.

Pfaff, W; Hensen, B. J; Bernien, H; Van Dam, S. B; Blok, M. S; Taminiau, T. H; Tiggelman, M. J; Schouten, R. N; Markham, M; Twitchen, D. J; Hanson, R (May 29, 2014). "Unconditional quantum teleportation between distant solid-state quantum bits". Science. 345 (6196): 532–535. arXiv:1404.4369. Bibcode:2014Sci...345..532P. doi:10.1126/science.1253512. PMID 25082696. S2CID 2190249.

Staff. "New largest number factored on a quantum device is 56,153". November 28, 2014 Retrieved January 7, 2015.

Devitt, S. J; Stephens, A. M; Munro, W. J; Nemoto, K (2013). "Requirements for fault-tolerant factoring on an atom-optics quantum computer". Nature Communications. 4: 2524. arXiv:1212.4934. Bibcode:2013NatCo...4.2524D. doi:10.1038/ncomms3524. PMID 24088785. S2CID 7229103. October 10, 2013

Physorg.com. "Repetitive error correction demonstrated in a quantum processor". physorg.com. Archived from the original on January 7, 2012. Retrieved May 26, 2011.

June 27, 2011 UC Santa Barbara. "International Team Demonstrates Subatomic Quantum Memory in Diamond". Retrieved June 29, 2011.

Grover, Lov K. (1996-07-01). "A fast quantum mechanical algorithm for database search". Proceedings of the twenty-eighth annual ACM symposium on Theory of Computing. STOC '96. Philadelphia, Pennsylvania, USA: Association for Computing Machinery: 212–219. doi:10.1145/237814.237866. ISBN 978-0-89791-785-8.

Shor, Peter (1995). "Scheme for reducing decoherence in quantum computer memory". Physical Review A. 52 (4): R2493–R2496. Bibcode:1995PhRvA..52.2493S. doi:10.1103/PhysRevA.52.R2493. PMID 9912632.

Peres, Asher (1985). "SReversible Logic and Quantum Computers". Physical Review A. 32 (6): 3266–3276. doi:10.1103/PhysRevA.32.3266. PMID 9896493.

Ekert, A. K (1991). "Quantum cryptography based on Bell's theorem". Phys. Rev. Lett. 67 (6): 661–663. Bibcode:1991PhRvL..67..661E. doi:10.1103/PhysRevLett.67.661. PMID 10044956.

Chapter 5

Coleman, Chris. Quantum Vendors. The Quantum News. April 7, 2021. https://www.quantumnews.dev/the-software-platforms-steering-the-quantum-revolution/

Chen, Shiyin. “Chinese scientists claim breakthrough in quantum computing race” Hindustan Times Tech. Dec. 4, 2020.

https://tech.hindustantimes.com/tech/news/chinese-scientists-claim-breakthrough-in-quantum-computing-race-71607074174517.html

Lin, Jeffrey; Singer, P.W. "China launches new quantum research supercenter". Popular Science. October 10, 2017. https://www.popsci.com/chinas-launches-new-quantum-research-supercenter/

LeBars, Laura. "Announcing the creation of the European Quantum Industry Consortium" LinkedIn April 9, 2021 https://www.linkedin.com/pulse/announcing-creation-european-quantum-industry-laure-le-bars/?trackingId=OMgREKG%2FvgJCokdyzk6pvA%3D%3D

Staff. "The revival of electronics: Programmable hardware for industry" McKinsey Digital. April 2, 2021. https://www.mckinsey.com/business-functions/mckinsey-digital/our-insights/tech-forward/the-revival-of-electronics-programmable-hardware-for-industry

Staff. "The Quantum Flagship: One of the most ambitious long-term research and innovation initiatives of the European Commission". QT.eu https://qt.eu/about-quantum-flagship/introduction-to-the-quantum-flagship/

Quantum Amsterdam. "€615 million for Quantum. Proposed, Approved, Action!" Quantum Amsterdam Meetup. May 12, 2021. https://www.youtube.com/watch?v=XcNkvs3Hgpo

Moore, Julian. "Quantum Technology Innovation Hub to transform local businesses". University of Birmingham. March 2021.

https://www.birmingham.ac.uk/news/latest/2021/03/quantum-technology-innovation-hub-to-transform-local-businesses.aspx

Lefebvre, Catherine. "The Canadian Ecosystem That Supports Quantum Innovation" The Quantum Computing Report. 2020. https://quantumcomputingreport.com/the-canadian-ecosystem-that-supports-quantum-innovation/

Kelina, Michael. "Quantum Warfare: Definitions, Overview and Challenges" Faculty of Nuclear Sciences and Physical Engineering, Czech Technical University in Prague, Czech Republic. Researchgate. March 24, 2021 https://www.researchgate.net/publication/350341569_Quantum_Warfare_Definitions_Overview_and_Challenges

Staff. "University of Maryland Launches Quantum Business Incubator" PRNewswire. Apr 23, 2021. https://www.prnewswire.com/news-releases/university-of-maryland-launches-quantum-business-incubator-301276142.html

Staff. Creative Destruction Lab. https://www.creativedestructionlab.com/streams/quantum/

Editorial Staff. "Germany to invest €2bn in building first quantum computer. Engineering & Technology. May 11, 2021 https://eandt.theiet.org/content/articles/2021/05/germany-to-invest-2bn-in-building-first-quantum-computer/

Kurek, Michael. Quantum Computing Patents by Country. LinkedIn. https://www.linkedin.com/posts/michelkurek_quantumcomputing-quantumcomputers-quantum-activity-6797680104647495680-URln/

Smith, Adam Oliver. “Finland is at the forefront of innovation”: the Indian-origin scientist managing the construction of Finland’s first quantum computer” Helsinki Times. May 9, 2021 https://www.helsinkitimes.fi/business/19198-finland-is-at-the-forefront-of-innovation-the-indian-origin-scientist-managing-the-construction-of-finland-s-first-quantum-computer.html

Walsh, Bryan. “Air Force research taps quantum computing” Axios. Apr 27, 2021 https://www.axios.com/qc-ware-air-force-research-laboratory-quantum-computer-3d038a18-e36f-40e0-9315-d18e9b174b61.html

Chapter 6

Staff. “20 Years of Quantum Computing Growth“ MBT Mag. May 7th, 2019 https://www.mbtmag.com/home/article/13251279/20-years-of-quantum-computing-growth

Feldman, Sarah. “20 Years of Quantum Computing Growth“ Statista. May 6, 2019. https://www.statista.com/chart/17896/quantum-computing-developments/

Qiskit. “What Is Quantum Volume, Anyway?” Medium. Aug 20, 2020 https://medium.com/qiskit/what-is-quantum-volume-anyway-a4dff801c36f

Dignan, Larry. “IonQ introduces Algorithmic Qubits to counter Quantum Volume in quantum computing” ZDNet. Dec. 9, 2020. https://www.zdnet.com/article/ionq-introduces-algorithmic-qubits-to-counter-quantum-volume-in-quantum-computing/

Swayne, Matt. “DARPA to Develop “Yardsticks” for Measuring Value of Future Quantum Information Systems.” The Quantum

Daily. April 3, 2021
https://thequantumdaily.com/2021/04/03/darpa-to-develop-yardsticks-for-measuring-value-of-future-quantum-information-systems/

BCG Quantum Computing Report, Exhibit 1 - Companies assume four roles across layers of the stack in the quantum computing ecosystem

https://dspace.mit.edu/handle/1721.1/124065

Shiyin Chen "Chinese Scientists Claim Breakthrough in Quantum Computing Race" Science Magazine paper December 3, 2020
https://www.bloomberg.com/news/articles/2020-12-04/chinese-scientists-claim-breakthrough-in-quantum-computing-race

Chad Rigetti. LinkedIn Profile.
https://www.linkedin.com/in/chad-rigetti-9891562/
Alan Baratz. LinkedIn Profile.
https://www.linkedin.com/in/alan-baratz-799b786/
Tony Uttley. LinkedIn Profile.
https://www.linkedin.com/in/tony-uttley-8597667/

Peter Chapman. LinkedIn Profile

https://www.linkedin.com/in/peterhchapman/

Chris Savoie. LinkedIn Profile

https://www.linkedin.com/in/chsavoie/

Robin Li. LinkedIn Profile.

https://en.wikipedia.org/wiki/Robin_Li

Eric Xu. LinkedIn Profile.

https://en.wikipedia.org/wiki/Eric_Xu

Kurek, Michael. Infographic. LinkedIn https://www.linkedin.com/posts/michelkurek_quantumtechnologies-quantum-quantumcomputing-activity-6793254220536528897-L_Us

Chapter 7

Microsoft. Flight Simulator. https://www.microsoft.com/en-us/p/microsoft-flight-simulator-standard/9nxn8gf8n9ht?activetab=pivot%3aregionofcompareeditionstab

Periodic Table of Elements. Ptable.com https://ptable.com/#Properties

Wikipedia. Quantum Simulator. https://en.wikipedia.org/wiki/Quantum_simulator

Staff. "IonQ performs the first quantum computer simulation of the water molecule." IonQ. February 26, 2019 https://ionq.com/news/february-26-2019

Hackett, Robert. "IBM plans a huge leap in superfast quantum computing by 2023" Fortune. September 15, 2020 https://fortune.com/2020/09/15/ibm-quantum-computer-1-million-qubits-by-2030/

Doug Finke. "Google Goal: Build an Error Corrected Computer with 1 Million Physical Qubits by the End of the Decade" Quantum Computing Report.

https://quantumcomputingreport.com/google-goal-error-corrected-computer-with-1-million-physical-qubits-by-the-end-of-the-decade/

Moore, Ben. "Pawsey supercomputer set to integrate diamond quantum accelerator" CRN. Mar 24, 2021. https://www.crn.com.au/news/pawsey-supercomputer-set-to-integrate-diamond-quantum-accelerator-562530

"Quantum Computers Approach Milestone for Boson Sampling" Physics 12, s146. December 18, 2019 https://physics.aps.org/articles/v12/s146

https://quantumcomputingreport.com/nvidia-announces-sdk-for-quantum-simulation-on-gpus/

Chapter 8

Taulli, Tom. "Quantum Computing: What Does It Mean For AI (Artificial Intelligence)?" Forbes. Aug 14, 2020 https://www.forbes.com/sites/tomtaulli/2020/08/14/quantum-computing-what-does-it-mean-for-ai-artificial-intelligence/?sh=276e81ce3b4c

Staff. "Cambridge Quantum Announces Largest Ever Natural Language Processing Implementation on a Quantum Computer" Cambridge Quantum Computing. Mar. 2, 2021 https://cambridgequantum.com/cambridge-quantum-announces-largest-ever-natural-language-processing-implementation-on-a-quantum-computer/

Staff. "Quantum Personality of the Year – Nominee: Ilyas Khan" Swiss Quantum Hubs. January 8, 2021 https://www.swissquantumhub.com/quantum-personality-of-the-year-nominee-ilyas-khan/

Easen, Nick. "When quantum computing and AI collide". Raconteur. April, 28, 2020. https://www.raconteur.net/technology/artificial-intelligence/quantum-computing-ai/

Wilson, J.R. "The future of artificial intelligence and quantum computing" Military Aerospace. Aug 25th, 2020 https://www.militaryaerospace.com/computers/article/14182330/future-of-artificial-intelligence-and-quantum-computing

Peckham, Oliver. "Global DataSphere to Hit 59 Zettabytes in 2020 Alone, IDC Projects" Datanami. May 19, 2020 https://www.datanami.com/2020/05/19/global-datasphere-to-hit-59-zettabytes-in-2020-alone-idc-projects/

Staff. "Volume of data/information created, captured, copied, and consumed worldwide from 2010 to 2024" Statista. https://www.statista.com/statistics/871513/worldwide-data-created/

Breeden II, John. "Will Quantum Computing Supercharge Artificial Intelligence?" NextGov. November 4, 2020 https://www.nextgov.com/ideas/2020/11/will-quantum-computing-supercharge-artificial-intelligence/169757/

Chapter 9

Sorbonne University. "Connecting the quantum internet." June 2020. Phys.org. https://phys.org/news/2020-06-quantum-internet.html

Welser, Jeffrey. "IBM Collaborating With Top Startups to Accelerate Quantum Computing" IBM. April 5, 2018.

https://www.ibm.com/blogs/research/2018/04/ibm-startups-accelerate-quantum/

Hilbert, Martin; López Priscila . "The World's Technological Capacity to Store, Communicate, and Compute Information", 2011), Science, 332(6025), pp. 60–65; https://www.govtech.com/blogs/lohrmann-on-cybersecurity/is-a-new-quantum-internet-coming.html

Levallois, Julien. "New tech builds ultralow-loss integrated photonic circuits" Swiss Quantum Hub. April 26, 2021 https://www.swissquantumhub.com/new-tech-builds-ultralow-loss-integrated-photonic-circuits/

University of Science and Technology of China. Researchers realize high-efficiency frequency conversion on integrated photonic chip." Phys.org April 23, 2021 https://lnkd.in/gXHjY65

Jia-Qi Wang et al, Efficient Frequency Conversion in a Degenerate $\chi(2)$ Microresonator, Physical Review Letters (2021). DOI: 10.1103/PhysRevLett.126.133601

Chapter 10

Staff: "Opinion | Even Physicists Don't Understand Quantum Mechanics" www.nytimes.com › Opinion › Sunday Review Sep. 7, 2019.

Sharma, Siddharth. "The Ultimate Beginner's Guide to Quantum Computing and its Applications". Towards Data Science. Jun 4, 2020
https://towardsdatascience.com/the-ultimate-beginners-guide-to-quantum-computing-and-its-applications-5b43c8fbcd8f

UNESCO Institute for Statistics. "Literacy rate, adult total (% of people ages 15 and above)" uis.unesco.org. September 2020. https://data.worldbank.org/indicator/SE.ADT.LITR.ZS

Hemsoth, Nicole. "GlaxosmithKline marks quantum progress with D-Wave. February 24, 2021. https://www.nextplatform.com/2021/02/24/glaxosmithkline-marks-quantum-progress-with-d-wave/

IQM. "IQM partnering with Atos and CSC to accelerate the commercialization of European quantum technologies" Jan. 7, 2020. https://www.meetiqm.com/articles/news/iqm-partnering-with-atos-and-csc-to-accelerate-the-commercialization-of-european-quantum-technologies/

ID Qauntique. "ID Quantique and SK Telecom unveil the Samsung Galaxy Quantum2, the newest QRNG-Powered 5G smartphone with even more embedded secured applications" 13th April 2021 https://www.idquantique.com/category/latest-news/

Quantum London. LinkedIn Profile. https://www.linkedin.com/company/quantum-london/
CERN. https://home.cern

Quantum Natural Language Processing Conference 2019. http://www.cs.ox.ac.uk/QNLP2019/

Skydive Toronto. https://www.skydivetoronto.com

LinkedIn Profile – Elias Fernandez Combarro Alvarez.https://www.linkedin.com/in/elias-f-combarro/

TU Delft. "The Quantum Internet and Quantum Computers: How Will They Change the World?" https://online-learning.tudelft.nl/courses/the-quantum-internet-and-quantum-computers/

Practical Quantum Computing: Virtual Event. Dec. 8-10, 2020 https://q2b.qcware.com

Universidad de Oviedo. https://www.uniovi.es/en

D-Wave Systems Inc. https://www.dwavesys.com

Elias Fernandez-Combarro Alvarez. "QTI Lecture Series: A practical introduction to quantum computing: from qubits to quantum machine learning and beyond". Universidad de Oviedo https://indico.cern.ch/event/970906/

Semuels, Alana. "Millions of Americans Have Lost Jobs in the Pandemic—And Robots and AI Are Replacing Them Faster Than Ever" TIME. August 6, 2020. https://time.com/5876604/machines-jobs-coronavirus/

Swayne, Matt. "JP Morgan Chase Unleashes Honeywell's Quantum Computer on Tough Fintech Problems". The Quantum Daily. July 2, 2020. https://thequantumdaily.com/2020/07/02/jp-morgan-chase-unleashes-honeywells-quantum-computer-on-tough-fintech-problems/

Lenahan, Brian; Qasmi, Mahmood. "Quantum Computing and Epidemiology: Research in the Time of CoViD-19"

LinkedIn. July 13, 2020. https://www.linkedin.com/pulse/quantum-computing-epidemiology-research-time-covid-19-brian-lenahan/

Lenahan, Brian; Ramos, Emil Sylvester. "Our Road Networks' New Partner: The Quantum Computer". LinkedIn. July 21, 2020 https://www.linkedin.com/pulse/our-road-networks-new-partner-quantum-computer-brian-lenahan/

Lee, Jaclyn. "Accelerating Organisation Culture Change: Innovation Through Digital Tools". Singapore University of Technology and Design, Singapore https://books.emeraldinsight.com/page/detail/Accelerating-Organisation-Culture-Change/?k=9781789739688

Greenemeier, Larry. "IBM Roundtable: Building a Quantum Workforce Requires Interdisciplinary Education and the Promise of Real Jobs" IBM.com. https://newsroom.ibm.com/quantum-workforce-roundtable

EdX. Professional Certificate in Quantum 101: Quantum Computing & Quantum Internet https://www.edx.org/professional-certificate/delftx-quantum-computing-and-quantum-internet

Wilson, Christopher. "Institute for Quantum Computing Impact Report - Building the quantum workforce". University of Waterloo. https://uwaterloo.ca/institute-for-quantum-computing-impact-report/impact-report-7/quantum-talent/building-quantum-workforce

Swayne, Matt. "NIST is Helping U.S. Organizations Prepare for the Coming Quantum Era" The Quantum Daily. April 28, 2021 https://www.thequantumdaily.com/2021/04/28/tqd-exclusive-nist-is-helping-u-s-organizations-prepare-for-the-coming-quantum-era/

Lenahan, Brian. "CERN Course Popular With Quantum Pioneers". November 22, 2020. https://www.linkedin.com/pulse/cern-course-popular-quantum-pioneers-brian-lenahan/

Staff. "Real quantum computers.Right at your fingertips." https://quantum-computing.ibm.com

Microsoft. “Microsoft Quantum Development Kit Samples” https://github.com/microsoft/Quantum

Staff. “The Swiss Quantum Hub. Think Tank and Startup Accelerator. https://www.swissquantumhub.com

The Quantum Daily. https://thequantumdaily.com

Medium.com. https://medium.com

Meetup.com “Find out what's happening in Quantum Meetup groups around the world and start meeting up with the ones near you.” https://www.meetup.com/topics/quantum/

Waters, Richard. “Goldman Sachs predicts quantum computing 5 years away from use in markets” Financial Times. April 29, 2021. https://www.ft.com/content/bbff5dfd-caa3-4481-a111-c79f0d38d486

Staff. “World’s Most Innovative Companies”. World economic Forum. April 2021 https://www.weforum.org/agenda/2021/04/worlds-most-innovative-companies?utm_source=twitter&utm_medium=social_scheduler&utm_term=Innovation&utm_content=05%2F05%2F2021%2011%3A00&s=03

Quantum Computing Conferences in 2021 - Waset.org https://waset.org/quantum-computing-conferences-in-2021

Conferences. Institute of Electrical and Electronics Engineers (IEEE) https://quantum.ieee.org/conferences

Conferences. Quantum Computing Report.

https://quantumcomputingreport.com/conferences/

Upcoming Events. Quantum Flagship. https://qt.eu/about-quantum-flagship/events/

Giles, Martin. "CIO Next 2021: 50 Innovative Technology Leaders Transforming Business for a Radically Different World" April 29, 2021.

https://www.forbes.com/sites/martingiles/2021/04/29/cio-next-2021-50-innovative-technology-leaders-transforming-business-for-a-radically-different-world/amp/

Chapter 11

Li, JA., Dong, D., Wei, Z. et al. Quantum reinforcement learning during human decision-making. Nat Hum Behav 4, 294–307 (2020). https://doi.org/10.1038/s41562-019-0804-2 https://www.nature.com/articles/s41562-019-0804-2?proof=t

Kobayashi, Yuri. "The IBM Quantum Challenge Fall 2020 results are in" IBM.com. December 16, 2020 https://www.ibm.com/blogs/research/2020/12/quantum-challenge-fall-results/

Staff. "Future of Quantum Computing in 2021: in-Depth Guide". AIMultiple. April 14, 2021. https://research.aimultiple.com/future-of-quantum-computing/

Khrennikov, A., Basieva, I., Pothos, E.M. et al. Quantum probability in decision making from quantum information representation of neuronal states. Sci Rep 8, 16225 (2018). https://doi.org/10.1038/s41598-018-34531-3https://www.nature.com/articles/s41598-018-34531-3

Taulli, Tom. "Quantum Computing: What Does It Mean For AI (Artificial Intelligence)? Forbes.com. Aug 14, 2020 https://www.forbes.com/sites/tomtaulli/2020/08/14/quantum-computing-what-does-it-mean-for-ai-artificial-intelligence/?sh=c29ff953b4c8

Staff. "How quantum computing could change financial services". McKinsey & Company. December 18, 2020. https://www.mckinsey.com/industries/financial-services/our-insights/how-quantum-computing-could-change-financial-services

Staff. "Quantum Computing: A Key to Autonomous Vehicle Industry Success". Futurebridge. March 19, 2021. https://www.futurebridge.com/industry/perspectives-mobility/quantum-computing-a-key-to-autonomous-vehicle-industry-success/

Staff. "How to capitalize on quantum computing (and avoid the quantum apocalypse) in your manufacturing business". Smart Industry. August 25, 2020 https://www.smartindustry.com/articles/2020/quantum-computing-quantum-manufacturing/

Staff. "Where robotics meets quantum computing - Researchers adapt techniques to overcome noise." June 17, 2020. https://cosmosmagazine.com/science/physics/where-robotics-meets-quantum-computing/

Chandna, Nikhil. "AI in legal industry — A case study on predicting judgements through deep learning". Apr 8, 2020 https://medium.com/analytics-vidhya/ai-in-legal-industry-a-case-study-on-predicting-judgements-through-deep-learning-4ca13f4cf8e1

De Schrijver, Steven. "Quantum Computing: The Certainty of the Uncertain" Who'sWhoLegal.18 Dec 2019 https://whoswholegal.com/features/quantum-computing-the-certainty-of-the-uncertain

Chapter 12

Skoff, Gabriella. "Transforming Drug Development: A Critical Role for Quantum Computing". https://projectqsydney.com/transforming-drug-development-a-critical-role-for-quantum-computing/

Terry Fox Research Institute. "ACCELERATE: Building the Digital Health and Discovery Platform". 2021. https://www.tfri.ca/our-research/digital-health-and-discovery-platform/accelerate-conference

Lenahan, Brian; Qasmi, Mahmood. "Quantum Computing and Epidemiology: Research in the Time of CoViD-19" LinkedIn. July 13, 2020. https://www.linkedin.com/pulse/quantum-computing-epidemiology-research-time-covid-19-brian-lenahan/

Delgadillo, Francisco & Montiel Ross, Oscar & Sepúlveda, Roberto. (2016). Reducing the size of Traveling Salesman Problems using Vaccination by Fuzzy Selector. Expert Systems with Applications. 49. 20-16. 10.1016/j.eswa.2015.11.026. https://www.researchgate.net/publication/287406531_Reducing_the_size_of_Traveling_Salesman_Problems_using_Vaccination_by_Fuzzy_Selector

Wikipedia. Travelling salesman problem https://en.wikipedia.org/wiki/Travelling_salesman_problem#Exact_algorithms

Stechly, Michal. Solving the Traveling Salesman Problem Using Quantum Computer. Medium.com. Mar 15, 2019 https://medium.com/@michal.stechly/solving-the-traveling-salesman-problem-using-quantum-computer-bb00438de223

Predictive Analytics Accurately Screens for Pulmonary Hypertension

Kent, Jessica "Predictive analytics accurately screens for pulmonary hypertension". HealthITAnalytics. April 22, 2021. https://healthitanalytics.com/news/predictive-analytics-accurately-screens-for-pulmonary-hypertension

Fontana, Carmen. "How Quantum Computing Will Impact Healthcare". Centric Consulting. Jan. 18, 2020. https://centricconsulting.com/blog/how-quantum-computing-will-impact-healthcare/

IBM. "Exploring quantum computing use cases for healthcare" https://www.ibm.com/downloads/cas/8QDGKDZJ

Chapter 13

NIST. "Status Report on the Second Round of the NIST Post-Quantum Cryptography Standardization Process". July 2020 https://csrc.nist.gov/publications/detail/nistir/8309/final

O'Neill, Patrick Howell. "The quest for quantum-proof encryption just made a leap forward - Quantum computers could make encryption a thing of the past, but 15 contenders are trying to prove they have what it takes to safeguard your data." MIT Technology Review. August 3, 2020 https://www.technologyreview.com/2020/08/03/1005891/search-for-quantum-proof-encryption-computing-nist/?truid=604e3ae10b5347c1f7f29d3c8d81aa48&utm_source=the_download&utm_medium=email&utm_campaign=the_download.unpaid.engagement&utm_term=non-subs&utm_content=08-03-2020

Galer, Susan. "Quantum Technology 2020 Trends: These Are The Immediate Security Threats And Opportunities." Forbes.

Feb 13, 2020
https://www.forbes.com/sites/sap/2020/02/13/quantum-technology-2020-trends-these-are-the-immediate-security-threats-and-opportunities/#5756460e6ac2

Dignan, Larry. "IBM aims for quantum computing safe encryption, security tools". ZDNet. Nov. 30, 2020.https://www.zdnet.com/article/ibm-aims-for-quantum-computing-safe-encryption-security-tools/

Staff. "Third PQC Standardization Conference". NIST Information Technology Laboratory Computer Security Resource Center. https://csrc.nist.gov/Events/2021/third-pqc-standardization-conference

Scott, Josh. "Canada Earmarks $80 million for News National Cybersecurity Network. Betakit. May 6, 2021. https://betakit.com/canada-earmarks-80-million-for-new-national-cybersecurity-network/

Prisco, John. "To QKD Or Not To QKD: What Quantum Key Distribution Means For Business" Forbes. Dec. 18, 2020.

https://www.forbes.com/sites/forbestechcouncil/2020/12/18/to-qkd-or-not-to-qkd-what-quantum-key-distribution-means-for-business/?sh=18dfeaff3e1c

Garfinkel, Simson. "Tomorrow's computer, yesterday - Four decades ago at Endicott House, an MIT professor convened a conference that launched quantum computing." MIT Technology Review. Apr. 27, 2021 https://www-technologyreview-com.cdn.ampproject.org/c/s/www.technologyreview.com/2021/04/27/1021714/tomorrows-computer-yesterday/amp/

Chapter 14

Gonciulea, Constantin. "JPMorgan Chase Prepares for FinTech's Quantum Leap." JPMorganChase.com https://www.jpmorganchase.com/news-stories/jpmc-prepares-fintech-quantum-leap

Staff. "Multiverse Computing: Optimizing Financial Portfolios with Quantum Computing". DWavesys.com. 2021. https://www.dwavesys.com/sites/default/files/Multiverse_Case_StudyVF.pdf?utm_source=hootsuite&utm_medium=linkedin

Staff. "Exploring quantum computing use cases for financial services". IBM.com https://www.ibm.com/thought-leadership/institute-business-value/report/exploring-quantum-financial

Leprince-Ringuet, Daphne."Are quantum computers good at picking stocks? This project tried to find out". ZDNet. March 15, 2021 https://www.zdnet.com/article/are-quantum-computers-good-at-picking-stocks-this-project-tried-to-find-out/

Finadium Editorial Team. "Lloyd's: impacts of quantum computing on insurance" Finadium.com February 11, 2021 https://finadium.com/lloyds-impacts-of-quantum-computing-on-insurance/

Staff. "Quantum Computing to Affect Insurer Tech Strategies" Insurance-Canada.ca Dec 4, 2019 https://www.insurance-canada.ca/2019/12/04/novarica-quantum-computing-tech-strategies/

Gasc, Jean-Francois. "Partnerships are vital to insurers' big AI ambitions" Accenture. 17 July 2019 https://insuranceblog.accenture.com/partnerships-are-vital-to-insurers-big-ai-ambitions

Chattopadhyay, Tuhina. "Business Applications of Quantum Computing". Mantra AI https://www.mantra.ai/blogs/business-applications-of-quantum-computing/

Wikipedia. Sortino Ratio. https://en.wikipedia.org/wiki/Sortino_ratio

Investopedia. Monte Carlo Simulation. https://www.investopedia.com/terms/m/montecarlosimulation.asp

Staff. "Is now the time for your company to investigate quantum computing?" HDI Global. https://www.hdi.global/infocenter/insights/2019/quantum-computing/

McKinsey & Co. "Quantum Computing Market to Reach $1 Trillion by 2035. Consultancy. https://www.consultancy.uk/news/24361/quantum-computing-market-to-reach-1-trillion-by-2035

Julich Supercomputing Centre. "Technology Readiness Level of Quantum Computing Technology (QTRL)". https://www.fzj.de/ias/jsc/EN/Research/ModellingSimulation/QIP/QTRL/_node.html

Baines, Stewart. "Quantum computing – next big thing or hype?" February 12, 2019. Orange Business Services. https://www.orange-business.com/en/blogs/quantum-computing-next-big-thing-or-hype

Staff. “Minimizing Financial Risk Using Quantum Computing” 1Qbit. https://1qbit.com/minimizing-financial-risk-using-quantum-computing/

Savoie, Christopher. “Why Quantum Computing Should Be Part Of Your Enterprise AI Strategy” Forbes Technology Council, Nov 30, 2020 https://www.forbes.com/sites/forbestechcouncil/2020/11/30/why-quantum-computing-should-be-part-of-your-enterprise-ai-strategy/?sh=1bb2a61226f6

Fortune Business Insights. “Quantum Cryptography Market Latest Industry Size, Share, Emerging Trends, Demand, Revenue and Forecasts Research Report”. The Cowboy Channel. January 14th 2021, https://www.thecowboychannel.com/story/43172853/quantum-cryptography-market-latest-industry-size-share-emerging-trends-demand-revenue-and-forecasts-research-report

D-Wave. “Optimizing Financial Portfolios with Quantum Activity” LinkedIn. https://www.linkedin.com/posts/d-wave-systems-inc%2E_optimizing-financial-portfolios-with-quantum-activity-6777277562184880128-XqTH

Investopedia. “Expected Return”. https://www.investopedia.com/terms/e/expectedreturn.asp

Lenahan, Brian. “Touring a Quantum Computing Lab & Museum”. LinkedIn. November 26, 2020 https://www.linkedin.com/pulse/touring-quantum-computing-lab-museum-brian-lenahan/

Staff. “Scotiabank gears up for the quantum computing age”. Finextra.com. 10 February 2020 https://www.finextra.com/newsarticle/35257/scotiabank-gears-up-for-the-quantum-computing-age

Staff. "Willis Towers Watson and Microsoft announce quantum computing collaboration to transform risk management". Intrado Globe Newswire. May 22, 2019 https://www.globenewswire.com/news-release/2019/05/22/1840831/0/en/Willis-Towers-Watson-and-Microsoft-announce-quantum-computing-collaboration-to-transform-risk-management.html

Staff. "Quantum Computing and Insurance: Overview and Potential Players". Novarica. Dec. 2019. https://novarica.com/quantum-computing-and-insurance-overview-and-potential-players/

Simon, Nivin. "5 Insurance Front-Office Processes You Can Improve with AI". MantraLabs. Oct 31, 2019 https://www.mantralabsglobal.com/blog/5-insurance-front-office-processes-you-can-improve-with-ai/

Chapter 15

Staff. "Quantum technologies - A potential game-changer in aerospace". Airbus. https://www.airbus.com/innovation/industry-4-0/quantum-technologies.html

Alqarqaz, Qusi. "How Microsoft Could Redefine the Power Industry with Quantum Computing". IEEE. Feb. 12, 2021. https://spectrum.ieee.org/news-from-around-ieee/the-institute/ieee-member-news/how-microsoft-could-redefine-the-power-industry-with-quantum-computing

Quantum London. "Quantum Computing Applications for Energy and Utilities - directory of articles and information — energy and utilities". Medium.com. https://medium.com/quantum-london/quantum-computing-applications-for-energy-and-utilities-a937d5839dfe

Cuomo, Paolo. "Industry applications of quantum computing". Oct. 24, 2020. Medium.com. https://medium.com/quantum-london/industry-applications-of-quantum-computing-fb21764b5dd1

Staff. "When CAE Meets AI: Deep Learning For CFD Simulations" UberCloud. April 23, 2019 https://blog.theubercloud.com/when-cae-meets-ai-deep-learning-for-cfd-simulations

Chapter 16

Mayes, Nick. "Is Business Ready to Make the Quantum Leap?" teknowlogy Group. 2019. https://www.sitsi.com/business-ready-make-quantum-leap

Lardinois, Frederic. "IBM brings its Quantum System One to the Cleveland Clinic" Techcrunch. March 30, 2021 https://techcrunch.com/2021/03/30/ibm-brings-its-quantum-system-one-to-the-cleveland-clinic/?guccounter=1&guce_referrer=aHR0cHM6Ly93d3cubGlua2VkaW4uY29tL2ZlZWQv&guce_referrer_sig=AQAAAIoJknJsj3vOyisWT46CuvzdTwRO2SGovgPsIOrftj8G79EzKnRB_hwF0X4f-_WNgW3D2ChQs_Lk12NrhZRVmpwSKyQ_x0wfyT-2pcj_gA_BDDX0hKDXewLGsSubX6kepaNoITeu7sqG34RbJscC-cnnyfPnFpVb2XOFlFcpmjTn

D-Wave Systems. "Save-On Foods". LinkedIn. https://www.linkedin.com/posts/d-wave-systems-inc%2E_quantum-qubits2020-quantumcomputing-activity-6719607529476816896-1gLq/

Shah, S. "IBM's first 'retail' quantum computer is headed to the Cleveland Clinic". Engadget. https://www.engadget.com/ib-ms-first-retail-quantum-computer-is-headed-to-the-cleveland-clinic-100152978.html

Mahendra Singh Bhamu, Dr. Mandaar Pande
"A review of Quantum Computing use cases in the Banking, Retail and Health sectors"
Symbiosis Centre for Information Technology, Pune, Maharashtra. 33764-Article Text-52543-1-10-20201127.pdf
mahendra.bhamu@associates.scit.edu,
mandaar@associates.scit.edu

Leprince-Ringuet, Daphne. "Quantum computers are coming. Get ready for them to change everything". ZDNet. November 2, 2020. https://www.zdnet.com/article/quantum-computers-are-coming-get-ready-for-them-to-change-everything/

Chattopadhyay, Tuhina. "Business Applications of Quantum Computing". Mantra AI https://www.mantra.ai/blogs/business-applications-of-quantum-computing/

Staff. Quantum Retail Case Study – Marks & Spencer. http://quantumretail.com/wp-content/uploads/2015/09/MS-CaseStudy_FINAL.pdf

UKEssays. (November 2018). Marks Spencers Enterprise System. Retrieved from https://www.ukessays.com/essays/business/marks-spencers-enterprise-system-business-essay.php?vref=1

Staff. Corporate Report. Marks & Spencer. 2019 https://corporate.marksandspencer.com/documents/msar-2019/strategic-report.pdf

Staff. "How Quantum Will Transform the Future of 5 Industries". Honeywell. https://www.honeywell.com/ca/en/news/2020/07/how-quantum-will-transform-the-future-of-5-industries

Staff. "The future of retail is here: Explore how quantum-inspired optimization delivers results for retailers produced by Fujitsu" NRF 2021. https://virtualbigshow.nrf.com/session/future-retail-here-explore-how-quantum-inspired-optimization-delivers-results-retailers

Chapter 17

Staff. "Intelligent traffic control with quantum computers". Volkswagen. https://www.volkswagenag.com/en/news/stories/2018/11/intelligent-traffic-control-with-quantum-computers.html

D-Wave. "Toyota Central R&D Labs: A Quantum Approach to Transportation"https://www.dwavesys.com/sites/default/files/Dwave_Toyota_Case_Study_V4.2F.pdf

Finke, Doug. "Quantum Computing Report – List of Startups". Quantum Computing Report. https://quantumcomputingreport.com/privatestartup/

Gossett, Stephen. “8 Quantum Computing Applications & Examples”. Built-in. March, 25, 2020. https://builtin.com/hardware/quantum-computing-applications

Langione, Matt; Tillemann-Dick, Corban; Kumar, Amit; Taneja, Vikas. “Where Will Quantum Computers Create Value—and When?”. BCG. 13 May 2019 https://www.bcg.com/en-ca/publications/2019/quantum-computers-create-value-when.aspx

Carrel-Billiard, Marc; Garrison, Dan; Dukatz, Carl. “Think Beyond Ones and Zeros. Quantum Computing. Now.” Accenture Labs. https://www.accenture.com/_acnmedia/PDF-54/Accenture-807510-Quantum-Computing-RGB-V02.pdf#zoom=50

World Economic Forum. “Global Future Council on Quantum Computing - Frequently Asked Questions” WEForum.org. June 2020 http://www3.weforum.org/docs/WEF_Global_Future_Council_on_Quantum_Computing.pdf

BMI. “Solving real-world problems with quantum computing” https://www.businessmodelsinc.com/solving-real-world-problems-with-quantum-computing/

Bowler, Tim. “How quantum sensing is changing the way we see the world”. BBC.com. March 8, 2019 https://www.bbc.com/news/business-47294704

Vernacchia, Simone. “Quantum leap - Advancing a strategy for quantum computing that will inspire, support and safeguard economic growth in the Middle East”. PwC.com https://www.pwc.com/m1/en/world-government-summit/documents/wgs-quantum-leap.pdf

Yahoo Finance. "Global Quantum Computing Market by Technology, Infrastructure, Services and Industry Verticals (2020-2025)" https://finance.yahoo.com/news/global-quantum-computing-market-technology-151854870.html;

"Quantum Computing Market by Technology, Infrastructure, Services, and Industry Verticals 2021 – 2026"
ID: 5236711, Research and Markets.com. January 2021
https://www.researchandmarkets.com/reports/4900662/quantum-computing-market-by-technology?utm_source=dynamic&utm_medium=GNOM&utm_code=n5rjsg&utm_campaign=1341544+-+Global+Quantum+Computing+Market+by+Technology%2c+Infrastructure%2c+Services+and+Industry+Verticals+(2020-2025)&utm_exec=joca220gnomd

de Boer, George. "What's on the horizon for the automotive industry in a post-coronavirus world?" Tomtom.com. May 14, 2020 https://www.tomtom.com/blog/moving-world/corona-automotive-sales/

Staff. "Volkswagen demonstrates first successful real-world use of quantum computing to help optimize traffic routing" Green Car Congress. 06 December 2019
https://www.greencarcongress.com/2019/12/20191206-vwquantum.html

Inoue, D., Okada, A., Matsumori, T. et al. Traffic signal optimization on a square lattice with quantum annealing. Sci Rep **11,** 3303 (2021). https://doi.org/10.1038/s41598-021-82740-0

Fujitsu Blog Editor. "How quantum computing could eliminate traffic congestion – and save 12 trillion yen in the process." Fujitsu. November 25, 2019 https://blog.global.fujitsu.com/fgb/2019-11-25/how-quantum-computing-could-eliminate-traffic-congestion-and-save-12-trillion-yen-in-the-process/

Chapter 18

Vizard, Michael. "Honeywell says quantum computers will outpace standard verification in '18 to 24 months'" VentureBeat. March 29, 2021 https://venturebeat.com/2021/03/29/honeywell-says-quantum-computers-will-outpace-standard-verification-in-18-to-24-months/

"Going atomic scale with quantum computing in the power sector" Mar 19, 2021. https://www.smart-energy.com/industry-sectors/digitalisation/going-atomic-scale-with-quantum-computing-in-the-power-sector/

Global Quantum Computing Market (2021 to 2026) - by Technology, Infrastructure, Services, and Industry Verticals - ResearchAndMarkets.com https://www.businesswire.com/news/home/20210120005456/en/Global-Quantum-Computing-Market-2021-to-2026---by-Technology-Infrastructure-Services-and-Industry-Verticals---ResearchAndMarkets.com

Mohr, Jakki; Sengupta, Sanjit; Slater, Stanley (2010). Marketing of High-technology Products and Innovations. Upper Saddle, NJ: Prentice Hall. p. 271. ISBN 9780136049968.

Swayne, Matt. "TQD Exclusive: NIST is Helping U.S. Organizations Prepare for the Coming Quantum Era". The Quantum Daily. April 28, 2021. https://www.thequantumdaily.com/2021/04/28/tqd-exclusive-nist-is-helping-u-s-organizations-prepare-for-the-coming-quantum-era/

Staff. "DARPA Announces New Program to Quantify Utility of Computers". Quantum.gov. April 5, 2021 https://www.quantum.gov/darpa-announces-new-program-to-quantify-utility-of-quantum-computers/

Staff. "Global Quantum Computing Industry". Business Insider Nov. 24, 2020. https://markets.businessinsider.com/news/stocks/global-quantum-computing-industry-1029835003

Lardinois, Frederic. "IBM publishes its quantum roadmap, says it will have a 1,000-qubit machine in 2023". Techcrunch. September 15, 2020. https://techcrunch.com/2020/09/15/ibm-publishes-its-quantum-roadmap-says-it-will-have-a-1000-qubit-machine-in-2023/

Greig, Jonathan. "6 experts share quantum computing predictions for 2021." Tech Republic. https://www.techrepublic.com/article/6-experts-share-quantum-computing-predictions-for-2021/

Glossary

"Appendix I: Glossary." National Academies of Sciences, Engineering, and Medicine. 2019. Quantum Computing: Progress and Prospects. Washington, DC: The National Academies Press. doi: 10.17226/25196.

Microsoft. "Quantum computing glossary". https://docs.microsoft.com/en-us/azure/quantum/qdk-glossary?view=qsharp-preview

Institute for Quantum Computing. "Quantum 101". University of Waterloo. https://uwaterloo.ca/institute-for-quantum-computing/quantum-101

Staff. Intro to Quantum Computing. Future Learn. https://www.futurelearn.com/info/courses/intro-to-quantum-computing/0/steps/47521

Staff. Glossary. Dot.Quantum. https://www.dotquantum.io/en/glossary/

Staff. Glossary. IBM. https://quantum-computing.ibm.com/composer/docs/iqx/terms-glossary

INDEX

Made in the USA
Monee, IL
04 November 2026

67384050R00144